SERENDIPITY

Discoveries Made While Doing Psychotherapy

By H.D. Johns

Note for Librarians: A cataloguing record for this book is available from Library and Archives Canada at www.collectionscanada.ca/amicus/index-e.html
ISBN 1-4120-6062-1

Printed in Victoria, BC, Canada. Printed on paper with minimum 30% recycled fibre. Trafford's print shop runs on "green energy" from solar, wind and other environmentally-friendly power sources.

TRAFFORD

Offices in Canada, USA, Ireland and UK
This book was published *on-demand* in cooperation with Trafford Publishing. On-demand publishing is a unique process and service of making a book available for retail sale to the public taking advantage of on-demand manufacturing and Internet marketing. On-demand publishing includes promotions, retail sales, manufacturing, order fulfilment, accounting and collecting royalties on behalf of the author.

Book sales for North America and international:
Trafford Publishing, 6E–2333 Government St.,
Victoria, BC v8t 4p4 CANADA
phone 250 383 6864 (toll-free 1 888 232 4444)
fax 250 383 6804; email to orders@trafford.com
Book sales in Europe:
Trafford Publishing (uk) Limited, 9 Park End Street, 2nd Floor
Oxford, UK 0x1 1hh United Kingdom
phone 44 (0)1865 722 113 (local rate 0845 230 9601)
facsimile 44 (0)1865 722 868; info.uk@trafford.com
Order online at:
trafford.com/05-0963

10 9 8 7 6 5

DEDICATED TO

Clare Elise

CONTENTS

PREFACE

I am not always aware of simple solutions to tasks so I have found it worthwhile to listen to other people. The other day I was having difficulty securing a panel in a door to my greenhouse. I had tried several times to secure it in the same way it had originally been secured, by taking the door apart and clamping the edges with the framing. Another person watched me for awhile and then made a suggestion. "In situations like that I have used an acrylic caulking compound." A light bulb went on in my brain. Why hadn't I thought of that? I thanked him, went to my workshop where there was half a tube of acrylic caulk, used it, and it worked!

In the same way, in listening to the troubled people I work with every day, I get ideas for monographs. I make a note of them on a 3 by 5 card and eventually get around to writing up some of them. Out of some five hundred of these ideas I present here sixty-five. I call them "discoveries" or "observations" or "solutions to problems." My main reason for writing about them is so that my children and my students will remember some of my thoughts and my ideas of how therapy works.

Most of the ideas expressed in this book are also mingled with the ideas of other people picked up in reading or in working with other therapists. My only originality is my method of expressing them and occasionally a turn of wording that I consider original. In fact I wonder if there is any new knowledge under the sun. Time after time, when I thought I had discovered something new I have run across a passage in a book, sometimes a novel, that speaks to the same idea. So, it doesn't seem quite correct to title this book "Discoveries." I have decided, instead, to use the word "Serendipity," meaning the finding of valuable ideas when not particularly looking for them.

I do consider these ideas valuable. Taken together they form an integrated system of thinking about people and life. Integrated but not complete. Innovations are forever being created, new terms take the place of old ones, new systems are being originated, and what seems innovative today may soon be displaced by something else.

My thanks is herewith expressed to all who have contributed to my thinking and to the formulation of the ideas expressed in this treatise. They are the thousands of people who have come to me for help and have often, unwittingly, been of help to me. My special thanks to Laura Van der Linden, my editor, who tried desperately to correct context and grammar. The errors remaining are the result of my resistance.

H. D. Johns
March 2005

WHAT I'VE LEARNED IN PSYCHOTHERAPY

THINGS I'VE LEARNED IN PSYCHOTHERAPY

1. STANCE (caring) is more important than TECH-NIQUES.

2. STATEMENTS OF FEELING are more important than STATEMENTS OF LOGIC.

3. HEARING is more important than PROVIDING AN-SWERS TO QUESTIONS.

4. MAKING AN OBSERVATION is more productive than ASKING QUESTIONS.

5. Every EMOTIONAL PROBLEM has roots in LOW SELF-ESTEEM.

6. Every OBSERVATION ABOUT ANOTHER PERSON is AUTOBIOGRAPHICAL.

7. ALL BEHAVIOR is CAUSATIVE IN NATURE. All behavior has antecedents.

8. The UNCONSCIOUS is MORE RELEVANT than the CONSCIOUS..

9. PSYCHOTHERAPY is essentially NON-STRUC-TURED.

    a. All structuring is the result of feelings of inadequacy.

    b. Some structuring is essential because of our inadequacy in dealing with the unstructured: such things as time-limits, privacy, fees, etc.

10. The use of AND instead of BUT creates a less defensive atmosphere.

11. The use of HOW or WHAT in the place of WHY creates a less-defensive atmosphere.

No Wax!

ONE of the obsessions of my life is to be authentic: as a person, as a therapist, as a teacher, as a parent, as a friend, in a world where it is unwise to be completely honest or open, and where almost all transactions are obviously or subtly manipulative. The search for authenticity sets up an inward tension that I must somehow claim as a friend or fight as an enemy.

Being authentic means that I do not attempt to run other people's lives or expect them to run mine, i.e., I do not discount the rights, respond-ability and capacity of myself or other persons. I hold as significant what I and the other person(s) are feeling and thinking and doing, even if a circumstance calls for me to over-ride their rights, respond-ability and/or capacity to make decisions for themselves. There are two such situations.

One such situation is when another person is actually lacking one of these attributes: a prisoner who has lost a right, an unconscious person who cannot respond, a non-swimmer in an undertow who does not have the capacity for self-rescue. In situations like that I am authentic even when I do decide to take over the responsibility which otherwise would not belong to me.

The second situation is when time is of the essence or it is a matter of life and death: when the other person(s) cannot exercise their own right, respond-ability or capacity because of the time-frame involved: a sailor just arrived in Hong Kong, starts to step off the curb while looking to the left, while to his immediate right a truck is hurtling down upon him. In that situation where time is of the essence I am authentic when I decide to pull him back or scream, "stop!"

Authenticity always involves decision. That is, to be authentic, I have to be decisive.

Authenticity also always involves a precise use of words. The words we use define who and what we are. This is graphically shown in the Chinese character for the English word, "sincere." The ideograph shows a shaft of the light of the sun shining on the precise spot, verbally, allowing the eye to look straight into the heart.* To be myself I must know myself and to know myself I must listen to the words I use. The person who says, "I can't," believes it. The person who begins a statement in conversation with, "Maybe this is unimportant.," affirms his low self-image. When we use vague terminology, we keep a subject vague; when we dilute our conversation with superfluous words, we dilute our energy to achieve our goals. The way we talk is the way we is!

Being authentic demands that I accept who I am, without attempting to change the things about me that cannot be changed. More, it demands that I do not fool myself by telling myself that I have shortcomings that I do not have, or that I do not have handicaps that I know I have. Every human being has handicaps. Whether I reveal a concealed handicap to another person is a matter of decision. The important point is that I do not deny the handicap to myself.

In Greek and Roman statuary, there was a term that distinguished the work of the masters from the work of others: "sans cera." It means, "no wax." Inferior sculptors could fill in the errors and rough places of their work with wax. The master artist used no wax to cover the blemishes. Hence, his sculpture was displayed "sans cera," no wax. That did not mean there were no blemishes; what blemishes there were, were not covered by wax.

So the acceptance of myself, without wax, presents an authentic person to myself and forms the basis for authentic relationships with other people. Those relationships are carried on without discount and with clarity because I hide nothing except by decisions, and the decisions are based on a knowledge of who and what I am.

Being authentic invites intimacy in a relationship even though the relationship be brief and passing. Authenticity invites authenticity. So the value is clear in establishing and maintaining relationships.

There is another reason for my interest in being authentic. Underlying my obsession for authenticity there is my own need to be accepted. Just as I am, no wax!

---

*Translation from Ezra Pound, Confucius The Great Digest and Wobbling Pivot, (New York: New Directions, 1951) pp. 20ff

ULTIMATE GOALS
(OF PSYCHOTHERAPY)

I believe there are two ultimate goals in all psychotherapy. There are, of course, many goals along the way: learning that I am lovable and capable, self acceptance, discovering that it is OK to feel anything I feel, uncovering my weaknesses and my strengths, etc. But the ultimate goals of psychotherapy are so important that they should be kept in mind by all psychotherapists.

The first time I heard the first of these enunciated it was by Mary Goulding, Co-director of the Western Institute for Group and Family Therapy: that one come to a compassionate understanding of one's parents. To that I add, and to a compassionate understanding of other people and of one's self. Why do people behave brutally or with indifference to one another? When we come to recognize that it is because they are afraid, we begin to understand them not as criminals but as victims of their own fears. Seeing parents and other people and ourselves in that way, with compassionate understanding, reduces the blame we tend to place on past behavior of ourselves and others and turns us toward changing our future behavior.

The second ultimate goal has been enunciated by thousands of therapists, both amateur and professional, in the past thirty years: that one needs to take charge of one's own life. In its essence this means that we make decisions about everything that is important in our lives. Most people live their lives without making any decisions. They grow up, get married, have children, buy cars and houses, and die without deciding to do any of those things. Either they do what they do because they think it is "the way to do things," or to avoid painful situations, or they do what they do in defiance of societal rules. These people are over-adaptive or defiant and both types are being controlled from sources imported from without. The defiant person, who resists all suggestions, is being controlled by others every bit as much as the over-adaptive person.

When I come to an awareness that I am responsible for my own behavior, no matter what the causes of that behavior, and that I have the right and the capacity to take charge of my own life, it is like a breath of fresh air that sweeps over me. I am inspired to make decisions and change my destiny. So long as I blame others for my problems, I refuse to take responsibility for changing them. When I discover that I am responsible, no matter who is to blame, I begin to consider alternative ways of managing my life and make decisions about every important element in it.

Without the ultimate goal of compassionate understanding therapy tends to become a treadmill of unresolved blaming of the past behavior of our parents, other people and ourselves. Without the ultimate goal of autonomy therapy tends to breed dependency on the therapist and/or other people.

With these two goals constantly in mind, the therapist develops a trust in his patient's capacity to heal himself and avoids the pitfalls of trying to reassure and coach the patient into "feeling better," enabling the patient to become responsible for his own behavior.

Principles of Assertive Communication

Since anger is always defensive in nature, in fact, a screen for fear, it follows that a major way to deal with anger in other people is to use communication techniques that reduce defensive behavior by reducing the threat that is perceived. The principles of communication outlined here tend to reduce fear/threat in the people we talk with. Using these principles, communication can be carried on with a minimum of misunderstanding, and open doors can be maintained for the exchange of information.

The essentials of the communication techniques suggested here are:

- A philosophy
- A stance
- Six keys to keep communication doors open

A Philosophy for Communication

I - Rt + Rsd + C to make decisions + TCOL

The first essential is: acceptance of the fact that every person, the individual (I), has the necessary attributes for successful communication. These attributes are: the Right (R); the Respond-ability (Rsd); and the Capacity (C) to make decisions and Take Charge of his/her Own Life (TCOL.)

You do not have to believe this philosophy. You do have to accept it as fact, and act on it, if your communication is to reduce to a minimum the amount of threat. When we see other people or ourselves as lacking one or more of these attributes we invite hostile behavior that defends instead of behavior that hears and responds. Discounting a person's right to make decisions disenfranchises that person in some area of his/her life. Discounting respond-ability declares the person to be irresponsible and reactive. When we discount capacity, we take on the impossible responsibility of doing the other person's thinking and deciding.

A STANCE FOR COMMUNICATION

The stance is the general manner in which you approach the process of communicating. Think of the stance as a four-legged stool on which you sit to talk with another person. Each leg supports the process:

- Do not contest!
- Do not dilute reality!
- Do assert your selfness!
- Do let the other person know you care!

Don't argue with another person about anything. Arguments seldom solve issues. If you convince another person "against his will, he will be of the same opinion still." Succinctly reflect back the feeling and/or content of what the other person has said and then proceed with communicating the issue.

Don't dilute reality. Do not act as though something is correct if you do not perceive it as correct. Do not take responsibility that rightfully belongs to another person; do not refuse responsibility that is rightfully yours.

Assert your selfness. You have a right and also a responsibility to decide to let the other person know certain things about your position. Asserting your selfness does not mean asserting your self. Assertiveness is not hostile in nature unless you decide it must be, and hostile assertiveness is truly assertive only when time is of the essence or when it is a matter of life and death. The difference in asserting selfness and asserting self is the difference between being assertive and being aggressive. Aggressiveness is a synonym for hostile behavior. It is much prized in games such as baseball or competitive salesmanship. It is destructive in human relationships. Assertiveness is the communication of your own needs or desires when you decide to do so.

Let the other person know you care. It is important for you to discover that you do care. In working with people for many years I have never met a person who doesn't care. "I don't care!" is a phrase used in anger to cover the feeling that I do care. So, two little boys playing with a ball: the first one says, "Give me the ball." The second one says, "No, it's my ball." The first one comes back with, "You won't give it to me so I'm going home." The second one says, "I don't care if you do." The first one replies, "I don't care either." Do they care? Of course they do. In fact, "I don't care" can usually be interepreted to mean, "I do care."

Caring is essential to communication. Studies of successful psychotherapy (essentially a process of hearing and being heard) stress the importance of communicating caring.

AN EXAMPLE OF STANCE IN COMMUNICATION

Tom bought a radio from a department store yesterday, got home and found it did not work. He takes it back to the Customer Service counter and the conversation goes like this:

Tom: I bought this radio yesterday. It doesn't work, and I'd like a new one. (*assertion of selfness*)

Clerk: Please fill out this questionnaire. We have to send all returned items to the repair shop to be tested out. It will take about two weeks.

Tom: I understand that you have that policy—and—I'd like a new radio today. (*Tom is not contesting. He is not diluting reality. He is asserting his selfness. And by reflecting back what he has heard, he is letting the clerk know that he cares about clerks*)

Clerk: I can't do anything about that, sir. We have this policy and I can't change it.

Tom: I understand you can't change the policy—and—I'd like you to call someone who can give me a new radio now." (*Tom is not contesting. He is staying with the real issue, not diluting it by complaining about the store having a dumb policy. He is also maintaining his assertiveness while allowing the clerk to know that he is a caring person by reflecting back what he has said. His caring is clearer because he uses and rather than but*)

SIX KEYS TO KEEP COMMUNICATION DOORS OPEN

Here are the keys that open and maintain communication if it is possible to do so:

1. State what I perceive the other person is feeling. If it is anger confront with the fear/threat that underlies it.
2. Own my own feeling. If it is anger own the fear/threat that underlies it.
3. Describe the situation in ten words or less.
4. Ask the other person to describe the situation.
5. State my "I'd like..."
6. Ask the other person to state what he/she would like.

Think of these six keys as six possible ways to keep threat at a minimum and maintain open doors for communicating. In a given situation, one or more will be appropriate. Sometimes they can be combined. Here's how Tom might apply them in the department store scene above;

Key #	Tom's Usage
#1	I know you feel you can't do anything about the rules.
#2	When you say that, I feel disappointed.
#3	I bought the radio yesterday. It doesn't work.
#4	Tell me how you see this as a problem for me.
#5	I'd like a new radio, now.
#6	What would you like from me?

In stating what I perceive the other person is feeling (1), use descriptive, non judgmental words. If the other person is feeling inadequate because of the pressure of the situation, my description of his feeling is not, "I hear you feeling inadequate!" Rather, it is "I hear you feeling frustrated by the situation."

By owning my own feeling (2), I do not blame the other person for my feeling. I simply describe how I feel. The formula is, "When you say/do..., I feel..." In using both (1) and (2) keys avoid confronting with anger. The very word "anger" tends to set up fear/threat. That is because, as children, we are taught that "anger" means "failure in relationship." The anger you perceive in yourself or the other person may be described as one of ten fear/threat feelings: feeling anxious, frustrated, overwhelmed, hurt, excluded, discounted, disappointed, feeling that it isn't fair, embarrassed or violated.

Describing the situation (3) moves from feeling to content. It must be descriptive rather than judgmental. Limiting this response to ten words tends to eliminate the negative criticisms that otherwise creep in. If Albert is driving seventy-five miles an hour, Harry might say, "You are driving seventy-five miles an hour." That is descriptive. Anything else added on to those eight words is almost certain to be judgmental, ("It's dangerous!" or "You'll get a ticket!") Adding value-judgment words also dilutes the information that is being communicated.

Most people express themselves more clearly when they use fewer words. A basic reason for that is the tendency to bring in irrelevant information, e.g., "You are driving seventy-five miles an hour, that's the way you drove last week, too." Brevity avoids entanglement. And almost always the extra words invite defensive (angry) behavior by being critical, e.g., "You are driving seventy five...don't you think that is dangerous on this busy road?"

One way of describing the situation when you detect that the other person is trying to get you to feel a certain way, is for you to say, "I hear you wanting me to feel... upset/stupid/ guilty/bad." Describing the situation in ten words or less invites the other person into a thinking mode. It is an enigmatic statement calling for the other person to get into his Adult ego state and think.

Asking the other person to describe the situation (4) is also an invitation to the other person to move into a thinking, understanding mode. One way of doing this is to ask, "How do you see what is going on between us right now?" That allows the other person to clarify the issue in his/her own mind and (don't miss this) may allow you to understand and appreciate a different point of view.

Demands, of course should be stated as demands, stated clearly and forcefully. They are useful when a bottom line matter is at hand. One such demand is a 7th key, omitted in the outline because it is used only when the issue is extremely important and the other keys have failed. It is some form of statement that puts the communication ball decisively into the other person's court. Whatever you use it should convey the message, "I am through with you so far as this issue is concerned. If you change your mind, you call me!"

An "I'd like..." carries no demand. In relationships, it is worthwhile to establish that clearly: "When I say what I'd like, there is no demand involved."

An "I'd like..." is an expression of my feeling. I am entitled to feel anything I feel, and I am entitled to decide to let the other person know about it.

Asking the other person to state his "I'd like..." (6) invites that person to clarify the issue in his/her own mind. In dealing with others I am entitled to know what it is they'd like from me. James may talk to me for an hour about a situation in the office or in his home and I find myself wondering why he is telling me. That is the time to ask, "James, what would you like from me?" or "James, how can I be helpful to you?"

The Assertive Communication Outline (page 27) sketches the techniques we have been talking about. It also speaks of problem words and problem behaviors.

PROBLEM WORDS

Two problem words and one problem clause are found over and over in miscommunication.

"Why" almost always triggers some defense in the person to whom it is addressed. That is because "why" is the second most frequently heard word of criticism when we are children. When addressed to children, "why" questions are usually unanswerable. In a thirty-minute period at Disney World, I heard the following unanswerable questions addressed to small children:

- A father to a small boy, pulling at his coat: "Why didn't you go to the bathroom when we were by the bathrooms?"
- An older person speaking to a little girl: "Why do you want another ice cream cone?"

- A parent yelling back at a child who has stopped to stare at Pluto: "Why aren't you keeping up with us?"

"Why" can start a meaningful question, and is often meaningful when addressed by a child to a parent. The problem with it is that we have heard it so much as children that when we are grown-up, we still hear it as judgmental and our defensive feeling is triggered. In many languages the word for "why" is the same as the word for "because" and "because" seems to fit our defensive mood when we hear, "why?" Question: "Why did you do that?" Answer: "Because!"

Any question that begins with "why" can be begun with "what" or "how," words that do not automatically trigger defense in the person to whom the question is addressed.

I teach the people I treat and the people I train to "scratch their 'buts.'" The word, "but" is often a problem word in the process of communication.

In the first place, "but" is a think-stopper. It is a principal word in the internal argument between the Parent and Child ego states known as the internal dialogue. When attempting to solve a problem situation by listing alternative courses of behavior, the "but" can stop our thinking either at the Parent level or the Child level. The Child expresses an alternative, the Parent says, "but..."; the Parent expresses a demand, the Child replies, "but..." In either case, thinking is stopped.

In the second place, "but" is a signal of a defensive stance. Usually it is used in give-and-take conversation as the initial word in a defensive statement. So, if you mention that I have, in some way, failed to keep an agreement, my initial reaction will be to think of a justification and begin my defense with the word, "but." Often "but" is used as a prior defense, a defense used before a statement that carries some risk: "I don't want to change the subject but..."; "I don't want to make you angry but..."; "I'm not prejudiced but..." But clauses used like that are like putting up the boxing gloves to fend off the strike before the other fighter gets in the ring.

In the third place, "but" when used as a conjunction, tends to place in opposition the two clauses it connects. It tends to make the two connected statements irreconcilable. Such a sentence seems to start out in one direction and wind up in another. So a mother, saying to her five-year-old son, "Bill, I love you, but if you slam that door one more time I'm going to put you out in the backyard and keep you there all afternoon," makes it difficult for Billy to believe that both statements: I love you and I'm going to put you out are true.

Except when the clear meaning of an observation depends on a statement of exception, "and" can be used in the place of "but" in our communication processes. "And" causes less defense-reaction, helps us handle our own defensive feelings, directs our attention to our true intentions and allows our connected-clause sentences to make sense. Whenever possible, scratch "but" and use "and" and your communication will be more effective.

Consider again the scene with the mother and her little boy. She wants him not to slam the door again. Whether he does or does not may well depend on what goes on inside his psyche when he feels unloved and defensive. "Billy, I love you and if you slam that door one more time I'm going to put you out in the backyard and keep you there all afternoon." The "and" brings both clauses together and makes them both believable. The "and" gives Bill a better chance of handling his defensive feelings in a constructive way.

"I understand," is a useful clause in communication when it is authentic and sounds authentic. It is more frequently misused to cut off communication. Often it is said with a vigorous nodding of the head three times and means, "I do not want to hear any more of what you are saying!"

PROBLEM BEHAVIORS

Quite frequently when we want to make an observation about someone or something, we phrase it as a question. A child falls, skins his knee and cries. His father says, "Did you hurt yourself?" Father has substituted a question for an observation. An observation does not have to be precisely correct to further communication. The wife has been quiet all evening. The husband says, "You seem a little down tonight." The wife responds to that observation, saying, "No, I'm not really down, I've just been thinking of how the children are growing up so fast." That is much more productive communication than for the husband to ask, "Are you feeling down tonight?" The usual response to that would be, "No more than usual, I guess." Observations make it easy for the other person to speak to what you have said. Questions are always more threatening.

This is particularly true when it is obvious that the person asking the question already knows the answer. "Harry, what are you doing with your hand in the cookie jar?" "Douglas, who pulled all the branches off the little peach tree?" An observation, even when incorrect, is easier to speak to than a question. Asking questions when the questioner knows the answer is perceived as structuring a trap, or a double bind.

When communication is flowing smoothly these techniques are not necessary. Even then, however, they may be practiced and will probably improve the flow of communication.

When time is of the essence, e.g., a child is starting to dart out into heavy traffic, or when health, self-worth or life is at stake, these techniques may, or may not, be helpful. Sometimes demand and compliance are required. In most communication, however, our goal is to reduce defensive reaction and to do that we have to keep demand at a minimum.

ASSERTIVE CMMUNICATION OUTLINE

Philosophy:

$$I - Rt + Rsd + C + TCOL$$

Every Individual (I) has the Right (RT), the Respondability (Rsd), and the Capacity (C) to make decisions ( ) and Take Charge of his Own Life (TCOL).

Stance:
- Do not contest.
- Do not dilute reality.
- Do assert my selfness.
- Do let the other person know I care.

Keys:
- State what I perceive the other person is feeling.*
- Own my own feeling.* (When you say (do)..., I feel....)
- Describe the situation in 10 words or less. (A camera view.)
- Ask the other person to describe the situation.
- State my "I'd like."
- Ask the other person to state his/her "I'd like."

Problem Words:
"why", "but", "I understand". **

Problem Behaviors:
Substituting questions for observation: asking questions when I know the answers; asking questions that begin with "why."***

---

* When ANGER is the feeling perceived in the other person or in myself, go to the underlying fear/threat which fuels it:

1. feeling anxious
2. feeling frustrated
3. feeling overwhelmed
4. feeling hurt
5. feeling excluded
6. feeling discounted
7. feeling disappointed
8. feeling cheated
9. feeling embarrassed
10. feeling violated

** "Why" is the second most frequently heard criticism when we are children. "But" signals a discrepancy in what is being said, as in, "I don't want to change the subject, but.." "I understand" is OK when it is authentic, not when it is misused to cut off communication, as it often is.

*** An observation, even when incorrect, is easier to speak to than a question. Asking questions when I know the answers is perceived as structuring a double-bind, as when a mother catches her five-year-old with his hand in the cookie jar, and asks: "What are you doing?"

JUST SEMANTICS

QUITE often, when I am teaching communication skills and insisting that the learner use a precise way of phrasing a response, I hear the student say, "That's just semantics!" I answer, "There's no such thing as just semantics!" The way you talk is the way you is! That is, there is a subconscious projection of our feelings and our communication stance into the words we use. There are at least four categories of words that stem from our subconscious awareness and reflect our feelings of low self-worth and govern our communication stance, i.e.,the way we are heard. They are words that dilute, words that limit the self, words reflecting grandiosity and words that are negative.

DILUTING WORDS

In this category are all unnecessary descriptives, such as really, very, actually, hopefully and surely. If I say, "It is hot today," it conveys the fact. If I say, "It is very hot today," we may take it to mean that it is hotter than hot, but how much hotter is it? If I say, "I am tired," it conveys a feeling. If I say, "I am really tired," it casts a shadow of doubt on whether I am or am not. ("The lady doth protest too much, me-thinks") Aside from the redundancy of the superfluous adverbs their use makes one wonder whether it is "that" hot, and whether I "am" tired, actually and really. Diluting words create vagueness and lead to a measure of disbelief in the receiver. Other words that aid in the projection of vagueness are phrases such as repetitive, you know, and do you follow me? often used in a message that is filled with generalities rather than specifics. All of these are usually superfluous words, extra words thrown in for emphasis or clarity, and instead of that, they dilute and obscure meanings.

Why would one say, "It's just semantics when "It's semantics" is sufficient? I think the just is a demeaning word put in to belittle the remarks of the other person. It certainly tends to raise my defenses when I hear it and that does not add to effective communication.

Add to these comments the fact that parsimony promotes clarity. To say what I want to say in the fewest words possible tends to make it easier to understand me. Often people who use these superfluous words give their message concisely and clearly in their first few words, then clutter the message in their ensuing words. Consider these words as recorded from a radio broadcast during the Viet Nam war: "There is a fierce battle raging in the Central Highlands--In fact, the battle now going on in the Central Highlands is without doubt, probably the most important battle in this campaign."

Self-limiting Words

This category includes those self-limiting terms such as shoulds, oughts, have tos and can'ts There are situations in which these words are valid. For example, you ask me to lift a stone, I try, it is too heavy and I say, "I can't lift it." And I should wear a raincoat in the rain, shouldn't park in a tow-away zone. It is when these terms are used as substitutes for decisive behavior that they limit our lives. So, "I can't stand it!" is a passive substitute for an assertive, "I refuse to put up with it.! "I should drive more slowly," is a non-assertive substitute for an assertive, "I'd like to drive safely," and "I have to go now," a non-decisive substitute for an assertive, "I am going now." The terms are self-limiting because they take away the awareness of the right to decide from the speaker and place the cause for his/her behavior on someone or something else. If I can't stand it, no one can blame me for what I do. I bear no responsibility for my behavior because I have no power of decision.

GRANDIOSE WORDS

Words such as always and never place the situation in a global context of conflict from which there appears to be no relief. If you always interrupt me, I can go on expecting always to be interrupted. If you never help me with anything, I have no hope of anything ever changing. On the other hand if I say, "You interrupted me three times in the past five minutes," I leave room for you to consider the reality of that as a fact and I have some hope that you will change. When I say, "Twice this week you watched television while I did the dishes," I invite you to consider what the facts are and I also invite you to change. Grandiose words leave no room for change. Citing authentic, specific instances by the number demonstrates hope and invites change.

NEGATIVE WORDS

Any critical or judgmental words create defensive reaction resulting in non-hearing. Think about it. You may remember the last time you spoke with a person who constantly makes negative comments. BUT do you remember what he said? Negative words reflect on the negative self-esteem of the speaker. Most of us prefer positive people to negative people. Most of us prefer up-beat personalities to depressed personalities and the constant use of negatives is often an expression of depression.

These four categories of words may be grouped under what Dr. Karl Menninger referred to as "static." He said that in spoken communication there is usually a subject and a predicate, and static. Static consists of all of the unnecessary words, the dilutions, the self-limiters, the grandiosities and the negatives that are thrown in because of habit and/or fear, plus the body language, which is usually more revealing than the words. Dr. Menninger goes on to say that what is important in the communication is usually the "static" because it tells us more about the speaker, his feelings about himself and others, and his communication stance than does an understanding of the subject and predicate he uses.

There is another category of words to consider: empowering words. Empowering words are positive affirmations about myself and others. I am, I can, I shall are the beginnings of positive statements about who I am, the power I possess and what I have decided to do. They are clear, precise statements that inspire the speaker to get on with her life. Sometimes they may seem grandiose in a positive direction. And Browning may have been right when he wrote:

"Ah, but a man's reach should exceed his grasp, or what's a heaven for?"

ON BEING PISSED

THERE are three main categories of feelings that we tend to repress in childhood because we are told that we do not, or should not, feel them. One of these categories is made up of certain fear feelings. That is, it is OK to feel afraid of some things: lions, speeding cars, fire. But it is not OK to feel afraid of other things: the dark, showing the visitor how you can sing the little song you learned, your swimming lesson in the big pool.

Although we are forced, also, to repress destructive feelings, we soon learn that the expression of some kinds of destructive feelings brings with it a temporary sense of power (along with a tinge of guilt because we have disobeyed a parental instruction). On the other hand, letting people know that we are feeling afraid brings with it a sense of humiliating shame, as though we have proved ourselves inadequate in human society. So in an average gathering of peers you will hear more open expressions of anger than of fear.

There is a common colloquialism that illustrates this fact: the phrase, "pissed off," which connotes some degree of anger depending on the inflection of the voice. That there is an intuitive awareness of the inaccuracy of that phrase is made clear by the increasing tendency to shorten it to "pissed." The ambiguity of that expression leads to a questioning of what it means. Invariably, when someone speaks of feeling "pissed," an examination of the situation reveals that the person feels "pissed on," i.e., threatened in some way (with accompanying fear).

It seems obvious that, just as anger is a screen for fear, so the meaningless phrase, "pissed off," is a way of covering a meaningful, and uncomfortable feeling of being pissed upon. It goes without saying that such an experience would be an extreme threat to one's self-esteem. So, it is more comfortable for me to be the aggressor and speak of being "pissed off," than to admit the threat I feel in being "pissed on." The underlying discomfort with, a distortion in reporting, leads to the ambiguous expression, "...pissed..."

Check it out. The next time you hear a friend speaking of being "pissed off," or just "pissed," say, "It sounds more like you are feeling "pissed on." Your friend will look a little surprised, then thoughtful for a moment, and then admit that your observation is probably right!

Underneath every "pissed off" there is a "pissed on." Underneath every anger there is a fear that fuels it.

FACTS ABOUT FEELINGS

THE process of therapy involves certain beliefs about the nature of feelings both in the therapist and in the one receiving therapy. My work with individuals and groups during the past thirty-five years has consistently forced me to concentrate on feeling (affect) and how it effects our lives. In that time I have come to believe certain things about feeling.. I call these things facts although it would be more correct to say that these are things I think I know.

1. Everybody Feels. For years popular psychology has been dividing human beings into two types: people who feel and, people who think. It may be true that not everyone thinks but it is not accurate to say that there are those who do not feel. The stimulus for one's behavior comes initially from feeling. In fact, except perhaps for certain obsessive-compulsive behavior, feeling always precedes thinking and behavior.

I believe that there are two basic feelings: Fear and Hope, from which issue thousands of nuances. There have been attempts to classify feelings into major categories, the most accepted being that of Muriel James (Born to Win, 1981) who perceived four basic types which she labeled sad, glad, mad and afraid. I consider glad to be a nuance of Hope, mad and afraid to be subsumed under Fear and sad to be a nuance stemming either from Fear or from a combination of Fear-Hope. At any given moment every human being is being influenced, sometimes ever-so-slightly and sometimes in a major way, either by Fear or by Hope. Consider such a mundane thing as turning on a television set and see how either you hope to see something entertaining, and/or fear you won't. Or think of preparing a meal. You hope it will turn out well and you have some fear that it won't. Or driving a car, hoping to arrive safely and often some threats arising as to your safety. Usually fear is felt as threat.

When I feel threatened I am sensing some kind of danger to my person: danger to my identity, my self-worth, my wholeness of mind/body, my acceptance (appearance to others), my security, my very being. Threat is experienced many times each day but we have learned to repress the awareness of it so that our lives will not be constantly disrupted by it. As an example of a minor threat consider what happens when two people approach a closed door together. Each experiences some minor threat: who will take the power position of opening the door? Who will take the added responsibility of opening the door for the other? Who will appear to be the dependent one? Who will take the place of honor by going first through the door? What will the other person think of me if I go first? What will I think of myself if I allow others to take precedence?

One gauge of constructive behavior is to determine whether the behavior in question was fueled by fear or by hope. Generally it may be said that behavior fueled only by fear is destructive while behavior fueled by hope or more often by fear-hope is constructive. This is particularly true of angry behavior which is almost always destructive. Anger is fueled by fear: in fact anger is a vehicle and a screen for fear.

Everybody feels although many people are not in touch with their own feelings. They have become numbed to their own feelings. We recognize that feeling is always present in children. A child likes to wade through mud puddles, why? Because he likes to feel the wetness of mud between his toes.

For like reason a child will smear feces on the nursery wall. He likes the coldness of ice-cream, or the feel of grass or warm sand on his feet. The child expresses her feelings by laughing and by crying, by pouting when she feels cheated and by sharing when she feels loved. But very soon the child is told not to express feelings and that is often heard as "Don't feel!" In fact much of our awareness is suppressed by our parents and our teachers when we are children.

A little boy boarding a bus with his mother says, "Oh mother look at that fat man." And his mother hushes him, saying, "Don't say things like that!" He hears, "Don't see things like that!" Little Ralph comes in crying and his father speaks roughly to him: "What are you crying about?" Little Ralph answers, "It's dark outside." His father responds, "You're not afraid of the dark!" We are taught to not look at people, to not feel anger, to not feel afraid, to not feel sexual. The very fact of the non existence of information about sexuality in the child's home and the absence of genitalia on the dolls that children play with attests to the suppression of sexual feelings. All of these suppressions become candidates for our own repression and some of us wind up not being aware of our feelings. But everybody feels.

2. The Feelings in Two or More Individuals Differ in Degree and Not in Kind. This is to say that everybody has the same feelings; that they differ not in kind but in degree. This is the basis for true communication in relationships: that we can recognize what other people are feeling because we, ourselves, have had like feelings. When my friend tells me that she has had a lousy day, I know something of her feelings because I too have felt sometimes that nothing was going right.

When I talk with a person who has paranoid ideology I can relate to him because I, too, have sometime noticed two people close together talking, and have seen them look my way, and have felt that they were talking about me.

When I work with a schizoid person, I can identify with some of his feelings because I can recall times when I felt that I was just an object in a world bombarding me with stimuli and had difficulty discerning which ones I should respond to.

When confronted with a person with a sociopathic disorder I remember times when I was tempted, or perhaps succumbed to the temptation to break out of the acculturated framework of my society.

When I work with an agoraphobic person, I can relate to his fear- feelings of being exposed, of being controlled, and of being out of control. Because I have felt crazy at times, I can even empathize with his feeling of being crazy.

The basis for true communication in relationships is the communication of feeling rather than logic. This accounts for some of the difficulties encountered by a man and a woman in relating to each other. The woman tends to express feeling, the man tends to communicate logic. Both are important but the communication of relationship takes place not at the logic level but at the feeling level. So when his female partner expresses one morning on awakening, "I'd like to go to Williamsburg," the male gets up, warms up the car and says, "Let's go!" without exploring what the woman wants to do or when she wants to do it. Or if she complains of having a headache, his immediate response is, "I'll get you a couple of aspirin," without even asking her when it started or just where does it hurt. Men tend to ignore the feeling level in order to get to the problem-solving level of interaction. While it may be more difficult for men to break the acculturated habit (and perhaps the tendency to think with only one side of the brain) of thinking spatially, and of problem solving, it is not impossible for them to hear and relate to the feeling level of communication because they have the same feelings as women. Feelings differ in degree and not in kind.

3. Every Feeling Has Its Somatic Counterpart. Neurolinguistic Programming makes much use of the concept of anchoring, one aspect of which is getting in touch with a feeling and burning it indelibly into the psyche by touching a part of the body so that to recall the feeling it is only necessary to touch again that specific area of the body.. That technique can be used to bring into the awareness a feeling of excellence during a time of stress or discomfort. My experience indicates that the technique is more successful if the part of the body touched corresponds to its emotional counterpart. For example, where is elation felt? For me it is felt in a lightness in the central chest area. So when thinking of a time of excellence I could touch that area of my body, and in time of stress use the anchoring technique to relieve the tension by touching again my central chest area.

Anchoring has another use. When an individual has a recurrent feeling that troubles her, I ask her to describe the feeling and then to describe where she feels it in her body and then to touch that part of her body. I then follow a procedure that goes like this:

"Go back and tell me when you had that feeling before." (I accept any incident they bring out, even though it may differ somewhat from the original feeling.)

"Now go back to your childhood and tell me when you had that feeling as a child.".

"Who invited you to feel that way?"

"What was that person feeling?" (The purpose of this question is to allow the individual to discover that part of their present troubling feeling comes from what the original inviter was feeling.)

"What were you feeling?"

"What did you say inside your head at that time?"

"What did you do?" (This turns out to be the same pattern that they use today when they have the same feeling.)

"What alternative behaviors are available to you today?"

I then explain to the individual that she can re-decide her behavior. Re-decision is the acceptance of an old feeling without accepting the old behavior pattern that goes with it.

All of this is possible because every feeling has its somatic counterpart. Hostility is accompanied by a noticeable tightening of the lips, shyness by blushing cheeks, withholding by a stiffening of the spine. Intense terror may result in losing control of the bladder or of the rectal sphincter. Fear is usually felt in the pit of the stomach or in a sense of restriction in the chest. Fear of speaking or of crying is often felt as a stricture of the throat. Paranoia is usually felt in a looseness or clamping down of the buttocks. Stress is sometimes felt at the back or top or side of the head. All of this speaks to the value of understanding body language, but in treatment the individual with the feeling is the one who decides where it is located in the soma.

4. It Takes No Energy To Feel. Feeling does not dissipate energy. The automatic repression of feeling is what dissipates energy. In other words one does not get worn out from feeling. One gets worn out from trying not to feel. Denying a feeling does not get rid of it. It may put it out of conscious awareness where it lies in wait to rear its head or to complicate one's life by causing the phenomenon known as acting out. And this suppression and repression of feeling is fatiguing to the person.

Most of us consciously suppress our feelings because of two fallacies. We falsely believe that:

- Denying a feeling makes it go away and that,
- Identifying and accepting a feeling puts it out of our control.

As noted above, denying a feeling does not get rid of it. It may push it into some subterranean area where it causes us to act out. So the suppression of fear-anger is often the causal factor in a homicide or a suicide. Read the newspaper accounts of parent-killers or mass-killers and note how often the neighbors and friends describe the killer as a mild, even unassertive person with no previous outbursts or displays of anger.

The idea that identifying and accepting a feeling puts it out of our control is exactly the opposite of reality. Identifying and accepting a feeling brings it under our cognitive control. In fact, identifying and accepting a destructive feeling tends to dilute it. The simple act of stopping oneself in an angry act and telling oneself, "I am angry because I am frustrated, or disappointed, or feel discounted or cheated," tends to dilute both the feelings of fear and anger and certainly forms a basis to desist from the angry behavior.

Identifying and accepting a positive feeling tends to strengthen it. This is the basis for much of our present sexual therapy. To identify and accept a sexual feeling tends to strengthen it. A sexual surrogate may start out with the touching of hands and speak of that as a sensual (sexual) feeling. Then the treatment progresses to touching faces, and other parts of the body, while constantly reminding the individual in treatment that it is a sexual experience. That identification and acceptance of the sensual tends to strengthen sexual desire and sexual feeling, Notice that it does not put it out of control. Rather it brings it under cognitive control. Denying sexual feelings and suppressing them, on the other hand, can be a source of acting out, in the form of voyeurism, exhibitionism, or some other destructive behavior.

5. Some feelings (e.g. guilt, resentment, defiance, jealousy, concern) are feeling structures, i.e., they are intellectualized vehicles and screens for fear. A feeling structure is a feeling of fear that is changed by shifting it from one ego state to another. When the Child ego state is afraid it automatically calls upon the Parent ego state for protection. The Parent ego state's response may be, "It's OK to feel afraid and to deal with that fear in a realistic way," or it may re-structure the fear into guilt (in which the person beats on himself), resentment (in which the person makes demands on another person), defiance (in which the person takes a stance of "I'll show you!"), jealousy (in which there is a demand to get even) or concern (in which case the Parent ego state attempts to nurture or often to control the self or another person.) Feeling structures differ from true feeling nuances in that they resemble behaviors, and can be controlled as behaviors can be controlled. In other words they can be gotten rid of by decision whereas true feelings cannot be willed away. I cannot, by decision, get rid of sadness. I can, by decision, be free of guilt when I know the reason I feel guilty.

Notice that you can tell the difference between guilt, a feeling structure, and sadness or sorrow or depression, which are true nuances of feeling. You cannot blow on your hands and be rid of sadness or sorrow or depression. You can, by decision, be rid of guilt. Guilt is always a racket feeling, it keeps you doing what you feel guilty about. And guilt is the payment you make to keep on doing it. To get rid of guilt, think of alternative ways you could have handled the guilt-producing situation and decide what you will do the next time the opportunity presents itself. You do not feel guilty when you decide to follow a certain course of action. You may feel sorry that you made the decision or sad about the results of it. But you will not be haunted by that pursuing cloud of self-abasement which goes by the name of "guilt."

6. All Feelings Are Mixed Feelings. Feelings are never absolutely pure. Love and anger are not mutually exclusive. Neither are fear and hope. In all positive feelings there can be found traces of fear. Even in despair one glimpses at times a ray of hope. This is clear when you examine your feelings toward your parents. You loved them and at the same time you had negative feelings toward them. There are probably moments in every child's life when she wishes her mother were dead. There are probably moments in every mother's life when she feels sorry that she ever gave birth! Consider how you feel when anticipating a vacation trip: excitement and perhaps dread or at least anxiety. Or just going grocery shopping: part of you wants to go, part of you doesn't want to go. This even applies to the grief one experiences at the loss of a loved one: often (and most noticeable after a long illness) there can be detected a slight sense of relief.

In many of the incest victims I work with I see unfolding this problem of mixed feelings. The victim of incest feels embarrassed and usually repulsed, sometimes actually nauseated in the recalling of the act. But from whence then come the guilt feelings that almost always accompany the recall of incest. I believe that the guilt stems from the fact that sexual stimulation is almost always exciting and may be even pleasurable to the child. It is not the repulsion and embarrassment that prompts the guilt, it is the usually unconscious, but present, awareness of excitement and therefore the accompanying feeling that she must have invited the relationship in some way. At any rate we can believe that the feelings, even about such a repulsive participation as incest, are always mixed, never pure.

This fact is helpful in recognizing the dynamics of relationship. I can be very angry with you and at the same time care deeply for you. I can even feel lust for one and loyalty to another at the same time. When Joe resents Mary and expresses demand that she change, she may feel that he does not love her anymore. In fact that may not be true at all. Feelings are never absolutely pure, they are always mixed.

I have an exercise that I use for close male-female relationships that are in trouble. I call it the Resentment Exercise. In the first step I ask each person to express three single resentments directly to the other. In the second step I ask each person to express three single "I likes" directly to the other. It is interesting to see how even in the midst of resentment there are things I like about the other person. It is also interesting how often what I resent and what I like turn out to be facets of the same characteristic in the other person.

7. It is easier to change feeling by changing behavior than to change behavior by changing feeling. You can't decide to change a feeling and thereby change it. You can decide to change a behavior. You are in charge of your behavior and you can change it by deciding to change it. And by changing your behavior you can change your feeling. The withdrawal of an agoraphobic is due to his fears: the fear of being exposed, the fear of being controlled, the fear of being out of control, the fear of going crazy. In order to change those fears into hopefulness it is imperative that he decide to take some risks, to venture out of his room (which he does initially by coming for therapy), eventually to board an airplane, drive across bridges, visit a physician's office. He would not succeed by being forced to do those things. I can only point out that it is OK to be afraid and within his fearfulness to make a decision about what he is going to do. I can also point out the safety of air travel, the fact that there are restraining banisters on bridges, and the fact that so long as he makes decisions he is taking charge of his own life. Notice that this is all an intellectual process. The major way we deal with feeling is by intellectualizing. Intellectualization, so often frowned upon by therapists, is destructive only when it is used as a substitution for feeling.

In this sense, the process of thinking is a change of behavior and the process of deciding is a behavioral change. In the intellectual discussion about his situation I provide the sufferer with a certain amount of protection from his fears.

8. Feeling Can be Changed by Diffusion. We carry all of the feelings that we have with us and they are available to us by decision. That is we can dilute one feeling by bringing in another. This may be experienced passively. You are driving behind a very slow driver who insists in staying in the center lane. You are frustrated and escalate your frustration into anger. Then, suddenly you become aware that the other driver is a close friend that you haven't seen in months. What happens to your frustration-anger? It is diluted by another feeling, the feeling of caring.

In the same way you can decide to bring in another feeling from your storehouse of feelings. When you are sad you can recall a feeling of happiness that you had in the past. When you are tense you can call up a feeling of relaxation you had when you walked in the woods by a lake and watched a sunset.

Or in your imagination you can climb up to 30,000 feet and from that vantage point put the present crisis into a different perspective: the moment recedes into calmness as you see it in relationship to your lifetime or in the context of a world of people.

Or you can channel the energy from a fear-anger feeling into a new activity: write a letter to the editor or speak at a town-meeting about your grievance.

Talking about a feeling over and over again does not furnish a release from that feeling. Rather, it causes it to magnify. Speak of it once, to a friend or to a therapist and let that be all. Repetitive talking about a negative feeling is a sure sign that you have not accepted it as a reality. And non-acceptance means you are dissipating your energy in fighting it.

9. Trauma Can Cause a Change of Feeling. It is well known that a terrorizing incident can set up a fear that was not recognized before. So, a victim of a mugging encounters fear in walking a peaceful street where before, he was comfortable and relaxed. When I was twelve years old my Airedale dog died and from the moment I learned of it I cared deeply about dogs where up until that time I had taken them for granted. A death in the family often leads to a new awareness of closeness among the other members.

10. Logic is Not a Response to Feelings. I visited a woman in the hospital who was facing surgery the next morning for a brain tumor. She was incredibly cheerful but it seemed forced. I spoke to her about it: "Mildred, you seem unusually cheerful for a person who is about to undergo a major operation."

She replied that a (male) friend of the family had just left and had reminded her that she was in an excellent hospital and had a skilled surgeon standing by.

"And that helped you," I said.

"Not really," she answered, "but it reminded me that it is better to be cheerful than afraid."

"So you're no longer afraid," I said.

At this point she began to cry, spoke of her tremendous anxiety and fear of dying, and leaving her two children and her husband. After a few minutes of that she seemed genuinely relieved that someone had heard her true feelings and I could reassure her logically about the excellence of both the hospital and the surgeon.

Usually, men want to solve problems, remove the pain and the fear by a logical procedure. Women, on the other hand are more prone to talk about the feelings and explore the relationships.

11. Institutions Tend to be Afraid of Feelings. The reason for this is that the force behind all change is feeling, and institutions, whether they be governments, corporations, churches, schools or families see change as dangerous to their structures. Advertisers have recently discovered that the word, "new" is not productive of sales. Individuals too, fear change.

Why are we as children told that we shouldn't feel? Because fear, anger, sexuality and even love are perceived as destructive to family life. For the same reason the organizations we work for and attend are wary of feelings. One sure way of getting promoted is to "not rock the boat." and feelings do just that: they may foment problems.

So starting as most of us do, with our families, then moving on into schools and jobs, participating in churches and lodges and government, we are constantly reminded that it is not OK to feel.

12. It's OK to Feel Anything You Feel. Since you can't change feeling by willing it away you have only two alternatives. You can continue to try to get rid of it, thereby dissipating your energy in a futile attempt to discard it or, you can accept it, acknowledge that you have it, and in a sense welcome it! By accepting it you can make it your friend!

Feelings, even potentially destructive feelings, have a protective function. Ted's fear of flying can make him selective in the airline he chooses to utilize, his fear of crossing bridges can cause him to be attentive to his driving, his fear of being out of control can insure proper planning, his fear of being exposed can make him aware that physicians need to be chosen carefully and can allow him to go to shopping malls when they are less crowded.

It's OK to feel anything you feel. Accepting a feeling does not put it out of control. It brings it under your cognitive control. This is more than acknowledging that I have a specific feeling. It is making that feeling your friend. It is welcoming it, saying, "Hello old friend," whenever you feel it. Be it lust or fear or anger. When it is anger it is necessary to identify the fear that fuels it, and accept that fear along with the anger. Underneath every anger there is a fear-threat. Whenever and wherever you detect anger in yourself or in another person you may be certain that there is an underlying fear-threat. This understanding and awareness is primary in dealing with anger in yourself or someone else.

The ambiguity of the expression, "I feel pissed," or "I feel pissed off," leads to a questioning of what it really means. Invariably when someone speaks of feeling "pissed," an examination of the situation reveals that the person feels "pissed ON," i.e. threatened in some way (with accompanying fear-threat.)

Underneath every "pissed off" there is a "pissed on." Underneath every anger there is a fear-threat that fuels it. I have found ten specific fear-threats, one or more of which can be identified when anger is felt or observed:

- feeling anxious
- feeling frustrated
- feeling overwhelmed
- feeling hurt
- feeling excluded
- feeling discounted
- feeling disappointed
- feeling cheated (feeling it isn't fair)
- feeling embarrassed (humiliated)
- feeling violated

Some of these overlap but connote some shade of difference. We can use this list of threats as a handy checklist. When you feel angry, stop for a moment and run through these ten threat feelings. Which one (or more) fuels your anger?

To accept your anger, make it your friend, and thus deal successfully with it, it is imperative that you get in touch with the fear that lies under it. The fear is your friend and it's OK to feel it!

13. It's OK to Think While You Are Feeling. There is a tendency to divide people into "thinking" people and "feeling" people. This is a false dichotomy that has led many people into not knowing that one can be both and do both at the same time. The next time you are feeling confused, spell it: c-o-n-f-u-s-e-d, there, you have proved that you can feel and think at the same time! This misunderstanding often leads us into expressions of grandiosity such as, "I was paralyzed by fear." It is probably more correct to say that when we are afraid, our thinking processes become clearer. Several women who have been confronted by a rapist have told me of their ability to think clearly at that time even though startled and in terror. So it is important to know that it is possible to think clearly when we are feeling anything.

We are paralyzed not by our feelings but by not knowing that it is OK to think when we are feeling. This is the second permission that I can give one to incorporate into one's tools for getting well. It is to be used consciously and often.

All therapy takes the step of thinking. It analyzes the feeling, its patterns, (how it repeats itself in my life), its sources (where and when it became established in my life) if possible, how it affects my life and what alternatives I have for dealing with it..

In dealing with obsessive ideology, it is sometimes easier for the individual to reverse the order to, "it's OK to think," and "it's OK to feel when I am thinking" but this is because of the predominance of the sense of obsessive thought over the recognition of feeling. Permissions then become, "it's OK to feel," its OK to re-think when you are feeling."

14. It's OK To Do While You Are Thinking And Feeling. This is the permission that makes the difference in getting well or not getting well. Since the sources of our emotional problems are rooted in feelings, and since the most effective way to change feelings is to change behavior, it follows that it is necessary to do something different if we are to change our feelings. One change of behavior for most people is to begin considering alternative ways of behaving and deciding to do something. It might even be deciding to do what you have been doing by default in a passive way. So a dentist, after having followed his profession for several years because he had "settled for it," decided to accept it as his vocation "for the next few years." It made a difference in the way he felt about it. He even discovered that he enjoyed the profession on which he had now decided.

It is at this point that most therapy that fails goes astray: the failure to change behavior. So Babs feels like a failure because she has not held on to a job during the past five years and because she is thirty pounds overweight. She has a pattern of staying up late watching television and oversleeping causing her to get to work late. She says her work is not interesting. She looked at alternative ways of dealing with her lethargy, for example, going to bed and getting up early and doing some aerobic exercise. She never made a decision to change her behavior in that way and she still feels like a failure. Even a small change of behavior, such as getting up regularly at 6:30, might have had a profound effect on her feelings.

15. It's OK To Enjoy While You Are Doing, Thinking And Feeling. This is the fourth permission. It involves staying in the here and now. Most of us are sacrificed between two crosses: guilt about the past and anxiety about the future. It is true that most of our future anxieties never come to pass and that there is very little we can do about what happened in the past. We can plan contingencies for the future and we can make amends for some of our past faults and such decisive behavior makes a lot of sense. What we cannot control in the past and the future we need to accept as reality and get on with the here and now. It means that we sharpen our awareness of what is going on in and around us at the moment and accept it: our feelings, whatever they are; the feelings of others; and that we appreciate our surroundings: the colors of the sky, the shape of the clouds, the birds and animals that come into our vision, the pictures and books that line our walls, etc. Ted speaks of taking a walk every morning, rain or shine, and as he walks, the internal dialogue begins: ubiquitous financial problems, relationship problems, physical problems begin to assert themselves. "I stretch my arms above my head, take some deep breaths and look around me at the trees, the houses, the cars, the birds and squirrels, and I begin to enjoy being alive."

16. It's OK To Relax While You Are Enjoying Doing, While You Are Thinking and Feeling. This is the final of the five permissions. It was also called to my attention by Ted, who discovered that the release of tension was important to his well-being. Ted learned the Relaxation-Response method of meditation and resorts to that sometimes. Usually, however, he says it is enough to say to himself, "It's OK to relax."

This is the essential core of Permission Therapy: that the individual comes to know that it is OK to feel anything she feels, that it is OK to think when she is feeling, that it is OK to decide when she is thinking and feeling, that it is OK to enjoy doing what she has decided to do and that it is OK to relax when enjoying doing what she has decided to do when she is thinking and feeling.

Two Basic Feelings

WITH the dawn of the Age of Aquarius there came a recognition of a revolution in human awareness: the awareness that "I feel" has become at least as important as the knowledge that I think, and that I work. I feel, therefore I am! The importance of feeling has taken root even in the industrial and academic worlds. With a lot of fear-feeling those who run institutions and corporations have allowed their constituents to participate in groups and seminars where feelings are encouraged and substitutions for feelings discouraged.

Communication deals with the transmission of two kinds of data: logic (fact/opinion) and affect (feeling). Organized behavior demands an adequate amount of the former; relationship demands the latter. It is true that people related for centuries without any acute awareness of feeling as we recognize it today. It is also true that the human race thought for thousands of years before it recognized thinking, and that human beings worked for thousands of years before they knew they were working creatures. When the race became aware of thinking, it produced universities; when it became aware of working, the Industrial Revolution changed the world. And now we are aware that we are feeling creatures, and from that awareness we are beginning to perceive our universe in a different way: in terms of how we relate to it and it to us, asking ourselves how we can not only live together in a world of life and chemicals, but live together with fulfillment of our feeling.

It is a mistake to say that we should feel. Some people who work with feeling make that mistake. Maynard, a sixty-year-old man, is attending a weekend therapy group. His wife, also in attendance, is talking about how difficult her life is. Maynard replies: "I know, dear, but we all have to put up with things we don't like."

A group member responds to that with, "Maynard, you sound so intellectual. You aren't hearing her feeling!"

Wife: "He never hears feeling. That's because he doesn't feel!"

Maynard, (with tears welling in his eyes): "I think that's true. I can't seem to feel. I know I should!"

The mistake here, is that Maynard is feeling and is being told that he is not feeling. Everybody feels.

Several years ago I began to wonder how many feelings could be listed and how they might be classified into categories. My students came up with lists of hundreds of feelings and we began to experiment with categorizing them. The first category was easy: Happy, Sad, Angry and Afraid. All feelings do seem to fit readily into that classification, with one exception: Hope.

Hope stood apart somehow. It was a bigger concept than Glad or Happy, i.e., one has to have Hope to be Glad, but one does not have to be Glad to have Hope.

Then came the awareness that Anger is always a screen or a vehicle for Fear, and out of that came the concept of Structured Feelings. Thinking of Anger as a feeling structured out of Fear established the concept of Fear as a comprehensive feeling including a large variety of feeling structures such as resentment, indignation and concern, each based on Fear.

A word about "feeling-structures." My belief that all feeling is experienced in the Child ego state requires an explanation because there are certain "feelings" that are manifested in the Parent or Adult ego states, e.g., resentment, indignation and concern. These are not true feelings. They are "feeling structures." A feeling-structure is a process by which we construct a Fear feeling into some other feeling-manifestation that is more acceptable, more tolerable or more constructive.

Resentment is a specific mechanism which translates the fear of failing into the fear of losing, and puts the blame outside ourselves. That is, instead of dealing with the primary fear of our own inadequacy, we project the blame onto other people or situations.

Indignation anger differs from other angers in two structural ways: it is structured from fear/hope rather than from fear alone, and it is consistently decisive in nature.

Concern is an often beneficial and socially acceptable way of dealing with Fear (anxiety.) The major difference in the structured concern and the anxiety-fear is the ego state in which it is manifested, which in turn, affects the behavior. The feeling-structure "concern" is manifested in the Parent ego state while "anxiety-fear" is manifested in the Child ego state.

The result of these perceptions: the larger scope of Hope and the awareness that anger is always fueled by Fear led to the classification of feeling into two categories, FEAR and HOPE. Most of us do not know much about the subject of Hope, Hope has not been a popular subject of study. Hope has been overshadowed by its more famous adjuncts, Love and Faith. On the face of it, that is strange.

Consider this: It is possible to be long on hate and short on love and never know it. It is possible to be long on cynicism and short on Faith and never become aware of its effect. But it is not possible to be long on despair and short on Hope and not be acutely aware that something is terribly wrong in my life.

Classifying all feelings into two categories enables us quickly to examine our behaviors and determine whether they are being fueled by Fear or by Fear/Hope, (Hope always contains an element of Fear) and to predict with some accuracy whether a given behavior is potentially destructive or potentially creative.

The discovery that we are thinkers and that we are workers led to a prostitution of those attributes. In other words, in order to believe in ourselves as human beings we had to think and we had to work. So we judge ourselves critically when we fail to think or when we feel lethargic. We are not all thinkers and we are not all workers. But we all feel! Everybody feels! That cannot be prostituted. "I feel, therefore I am!

DEALING WITH FEELINGS

ALL people feel. Some people do not know they feel. Others know they feel but do not know what they feel. They have not identified their feelings. In these people some or all feelings have been * repressed out of their awareness.

When feelings are not acknowledged the result is called acting out. So an individual might act out an unrecognized feeling of fear-anger by habitually showing up late for scheduled meetings with friends or associates. An older daughter remains in the parental home to care for her widowed, invalid mother. Occasionally she accidentally spills coffee on her mother's favorite bedspread, or gives her the wrong medicine, but both mother and daughter believe that these are accidents and both would be shocked to discover that the daughter harbors a fear-anger about losing out on marriage and the possibility of having her own family.

Transference, the unrecognized displacement of feeling from one object to another, leads us into acting out. Transference is always present in psychotherapy as well as in most other relationships. As an example, the individual may direct upon the therapist or upon a friend, the suppressed adoration or the hatred he feels toward his mother or his father.

There are three main categories of feelings that we tend to repress in childhood because we are told that we do not, or should not, feel them:

- destructive feelings, e.g., the wish that someone will get hurt or die,
- certain fear feelings, e.g., fear of the future or of the dark,
- sexual feelings, e.g., the excitement caused by a sexual stimulus.

In the first of these, destructive feelings, a typical scenario might be one in which there is a conflict of the little guy's wishes and the parent's demands. Six-year old Ted wants to go out and play and his mother insists that he study his homework. "I hate you, mother, I wish your were dead!" Ted exclaims, to which his mother replies sanctimoniously, "You know you don't hate your mother!" The truth is that, at that moment, Ted actually does wish his mother was out of his way, even dead. But the very sanctity of his mother's declaration forces him to feel guilty and to suppress and repress his feeling. From that day forward he will feel guilty about any destructive feelings he has and he will tend to suppress any such feelings toward those closest to him.In the second of these admonished feelings, fear feelings, it might be that little Ralph comes into the house one evening crying. His father asks him why he is crying and he replies that it is dark outside. His father, again with a kind of holy tone of voice says, "You're not afraid of the dark!" And from that moment on Ralph feels a sense of shame for feeling fear of the dark or of uncertainty. So he suppresses it and represses it and denies that he feels afraid. He may also have learned that it is more acceptable to express his fear as angry behavior than as an admission of fear.

In the third category of repressed feeling, sexual feelings, it may be, as in the case of Ted, that his mother, on hearing a dream he had of having his penis examined by a doctor, exclaims with a kind of terror in her voice, "Leave that alone and don't ever do that again,." or it may be that sex is never mentioned, except in a jesting tone, in the family conversations and is left in the realm of forbidden mysteries.

Thus, many people grow up from childhood unaware of the fact that they are feeling beings.

The purpose of dealing with feelings does not mean that we seek to rid ourselves of any given feelings but that we establish control over it so that it does not influence our behavior in ways we do not like. In dealing successfully with feeling it is important first of all that we recognize that we have it. This means that we get in touch with the fact that we feel.

GETTING IN TOUCH WITH FEELINGS

At this initial point we are not so much interested in what we are feeling as in the fact that we are feeling. We can contrive ways to get in touch with feeling. Here are five suggestions that can help.

• Talk to your dog or cat or tropical fish about what she means to you. One of my clients had been told by a previous therapist that he did not experience love in his childhood and appeared to be incapable of giving and accepting love in his adulthood. He adopted a kitten and began to talk to it. He told me about the conversation. "I came home last evening and the kitten seemed glad to see me. She jumped up on my lap and I held her and stroked her. I thought about her being alone in the apartment all day and I told her that I felt sad about that. She began to purr, and I knew she felt secure and I said, 'I love you, kitten!' I really felt love."

• Touch someone's face and be aware of the softness and smoothness of the skin. Ask someone to touch your face, softly, just in front of the ear, and be aware of the sensation of that touch. Ask yourself the question, "What happens in my awareness when I am touched? What do I feel?"

• Lie on your back on the floor and talk to a friend/

spouse about an experience of the day or the week, or an event in your memory: the time you went fishing or played tennis with your dad; the time someone, father, mother, sister, brother was ill. Let go and let yourself feel.

• While lying on a carpeted floor, ask a friend to rub your back and be aware that you don't have to pay her back in any way.

• Put four playing cards, representing the four suits, in a shirt pocket or in your purse. Let each suit represent a different feeling:

> Hearts (glad) - hope, joy, gladness, love
> Spades (sad) - fear, threat, hurt
> Clubs   (mad) - anger, irritation, annoyance
> Diamonds   (had) - violated, discounted, excluded

At times through the day, look at the cards and place the suit that represents the feeling you have at that moment on top. Think into that feeling and acknowledge it.

Most people, of course, are already aware that they feel and with them this step is not necessary although it may be helpful in getting in touch with some feelings which are suppressed. A surprising number of people, however, are not aware that they feel, and for them this initial step is an absolute requirement for dealing successfully with their feelings.

IDENTIFYING THE FEELING

The second step in dealing with feeling is identifying the feeling. Definition may be as specific as you wish. At least you will differentiate between basic hope and basic fear. Fear-threats, all of which indicate a foreboding of personal inadequacy can be further classified into four categories:

1. The fear of failing,
2. The fear of losing,

3. The fear of loss of selfness,
4. The fear of injustice.

All fear is accompanied by anxiety. Anxiety is fueled by "the worst thing fantasy." So the way to determine the underlying fear is to ask a series of questions including, "What is the worst thing that could happen to me when I am feeling that anxiety?" and/or "What's so bad about that for me?"

My secretary at the Naval Hospital, Bethesda, Maryland, was given to making spelling errors in the letters she wrote, some of which were for the signature of the Commanding Officer, an Admiral. I knew this and the letters that went out over my name I often corrected with pen and ink. The letters that were for the Admiral were proofread by the Administrative Officer.

One night, returning from a trip, I stopped by the office and noticed two memoranda in Alice's tray. They were written in red ink which called my attention to them. They were both from the Administrative Officer. The first one read, "Mrs. M. there are dictionaries available through supply channels. I suggest you get one." The second one said, "Mrs. M., I am going to be at Supply tomorrow. I'll pick up a dictionary for you."

Sensing the anxiety of the Administrative Officer, the next morning I stopped in to see him. The conversation went like this:

I: I noticed the memos in Alice's tray and I'm aware that you are anxious about her spelling.

A.O.: Yeah, she makes a lot of mistakes.

I: What's so bad about her making mistakes?

A.O.: Well, the Admiral gets those letters.

I: What's so bad about the Admiral seeing her mistakes?

A.O.: He writes my fitness reports and if I get a couple of bad reports I'll be passed over for promotion and get kicked out of this canoe club.

I: What's so bad about getting kicked out of the navy?

A.O.: I've been in the navy since I was 17 year old. I don't know anything else.

I: What's so bad about being out of the navy and not knowing what else you can do?

A.O.: I'd wind up in the poor house!

One mistake in Alice's spelling and the Administrative Officer fantasizes "winding up in the poor house." His basic underlying fear was the fear of failing.

Mary is a fifty-year old divorcee who comes to me because she is afraid of dating. She is attractive and has opportunities to go out with men but says, "I'm just afraid to do it and I push them away."

I: "What's the worst thing that could happen if you went out with a man?"

Mary: "I don't know, he might want to hold my hand."

I: "What's so bad about that?"

Mary: "Well, you know, he might want to kiss me."

I: "What's so bad about that?"

Mary: "Well, he might want me to go to bed with him."

I: "What's the worst thing that could happen if you went to bed with him?"

Mary: (After a long pause,) "I wouldn't please him."

Here again is the fear of failing.

If you are dealing with a feeling of anger it is necessary to get in touch with the fear-threat feeling that triggers the anger. Roy complains about speeding tickets. He has gotten four of them in two years. He is angry with the police officers who gave him the tickets.

I: "What's so bad about getting four speeding tickets?"

Roy: "Man, it cost me almost three hundred dollars."

I: "What's so bad about throwing away three hundred dollars on speeding tickets?"

Roy: "I don't like to be told how fast I can drive."

I: "What's going to happen to you if people tell you how fast you can drive?"

Roy: "I want to be the judge of how fast I can drive."

Underneath Roy's anger is the fear of the loss of selfness, the fear of being controlled. Underneath his being "pissed off" he feels "pissed on."

Whatever the feeling you seek to deal successfully with, it is important to identify it, and usually it is one of the four fears: failing, losing, loss of selfness or injustice. They can be further broken down into ten specific fear-threats that are easily recognizable.

SURFACING THE FEELING

The third step in dealing with feeling I refer to as surfacing. By that I mean accepting it, but more than that. I mean bringing the specific feeling into the focus of our attention in an act of acceptance. Acceptance of a feeling is sometimes difficult to achieve.* Acceptance and denial have a strange similarity in appearance when dealing with feeling. I become aware of a specific feeling that I am uncomfortable with. My acceptance of that feeling is not achieved if I am trying, through my acceptance, to be rid of it! So I use the term "surface" because it suggests a picture of feeling emerging as a bubble at the bottom of a glass-enclosed aquarium. As the person with the feeling, I relax and observe the bubble as it rises slowly through the water to the surface where it joins with the other gases of the atmosphere. A formula I use in accepting a feeling is to repeat to myself, "Hello, old friend," meaning, "I have seen you many times before and I welcome you back as a reminder of my past and my growth.'

When the feeling I am dealing with is an anger feeling and I have identified the underlying fear, then the surfacing is an acceptance of both the anger and the fear and I accept them both. This acceptance of any feeling is the most important thing I know about as a therapist.

DECIDING WHAT TO DO WITH THE FEELING

The fourth step in dealing with feeling is a decision on what to do with it. There are four alternatives:

1. Expressing it by Acting In. When I identify and accept the feeling I can decide to act in on it. This may be either appropriate or non-appropriate behavior. To see how this would work, imagine that an impatient driver cuts you off in traffic. Your second feeling might be one of vengeance fueled by a preceding feeling of the fear of the loss-of-selfness. Having gotten in touch with the feelings and identified them you could act in on them, either appropriately or non-appropriately as a response to the feelings. Acting in inappropriately would be a decision to speed up and cut in front of the other driver. An appropriate expression would be a decision to slow down and let the hurried driver move ahead.

2. Verbalizing it. I can verbalize my fear feeling to myself and/or to another person. Verbalization would be saying, "I am feeling afraid and I am feeling angry."

3. Diluting it. There are at least three ways of diluting the identified and accepted feeling.

- The first one is Objectification. By this I mean that I fly up to 30,000 feet and look down upon the incident from that perspective. From that lofty point I realize that this is only one moment in my lifetime and that both the fear and the anger will pass.

- The second way of diluting is Infusion. I use this term to indicate the bringing in of other feelings in direct dilution of the feeling being experienced. Since we never get rid of a feeling we carry a varied supply around in our psyche. Without deciding to we frequently use infusion to control a behavior. So, in the example above, the harassed driver might control his angry behavior by becoming aware of a fear of what the other driver might do if angered. An improvement on that would be a decision to bring in another feeling, fear perhaps, or a feeling of being a responsible driver. An automatic infusion in the example cited above would be a discovery that the other driver is, in fact, your closest friend. The infusion of caring would dilute the anger and its underlying fear.

- A third way of diluting is by Venting. Venting, the discharge of angry feelings through ritualized behavior (e.g. stomping the foot) or some pseudo-hostile action (e.g. beating on a pillow) is a useful technique only when it is used by decision for the purpose of discharging the energy built up by the flow of adrenaline and the consequent release of blood sugar. It does not get rid of anger. It does discharge energy and allows the system to return to a quietened state.

4. Suppressing it. The fourth direction a decision about dealing with a feeling can take is suppression. By this I mean a conscious decision to lay the matter on the table for a given time frame. It differs from repression in that it is a conscious act. When done by decision, suppressing a feeling relieves one of the pressure for immediate action that emotion calls for. In the example above, a decision to suppress would mean, "I will attend to my driving now and consider my feelings in more detail when I reach my destination."

You might think of this process as a ladder. It is a process that I and many other people have found useful in dealing with any feeling. First, it calls on us to get in touch with feeling; second, to identify it, and if it is anger, the fear that fuels it; third, to accept it without trying to be rid of it; and fourth, to decide to act in one or more of the four ways that bring it under control.

We have seen how it works in a situation that has provoked fear-anger. It also works, when needed, in situations of positive and/or sexual feelings.

---

* Repression carries the connotation that the process of exclusion of the feeling from awareness is not conscious. Suppression, on the other hand, indicates that the process is one of self-control by which the feelings is kept from overt expression.

* Timothy, a man of sixty-two years, has a re-occurrence of cancer. On the first occurrence, when he was told, he denied his feelings of fear and anger. In fact, he told his friends that it was not cancer and went on with his daily life as though nothing was wrong. On the re-occurence, he changed his lifestyle. He began to play tennis, built a swimming pool, and bought an ocean condominium in Florida. Questions: Does his behavior after the re-occurrence indicate further denial of his feelings, or does it indicate an acceptance of his feelings? Only Timothy knows. But if it is denial he will be wasting energy on getting rid of his feelings. If it is acceptance, his energy will be available for healing.

Scratching Your "Buts"

I teach the people I treat and the people I train to scratch their "buts." The word "but" is often a problem word in the process of communication.

In the first place,, but is a think-stopper. It is a principle word in the internal argument between Parent and Child ego states known as the "internal dialogue." When attempting to solve a problem situation by listing alternative courses of behavior, the "but" can stop our thinking either at the Parent level or the Child level. The Child expresses an alternative, the Parent says, "But...", the Parent expresses a suggestion, the Child replies, "But...".

In the second place, "but" is a signal of a defensive stance. Usually it is used, in give-and-take conversation as the initial word in a defensive statement. So, if you mention that I have, in some way, failed to keep an agreement, my initial reaction will be to think of a justification and begin my defense with the word, "but." Often, "but" is used as a "prior" defensive ploy, a defense used before a statement that carries some risk: "I don't want to change the subject but...," "I don't want to make you angry but...," "I'm not prejudiced but..." "But" clauses used like that are like putting up the boxing gloves to fend off the strike before the other fighter gets in the ring.

In the third place, "but", when used as a conjunction, tends to place in opposition the two clauses it connects. It tends to make the two connected statements irreconcilable. Such a sentence seems to start out in one direction and wind up in another. So, a mother, saying to her five-year-old son, "Billy, I love you, BUT if you slam that door one more time I'm going to put you out in the back yard and keep you there all afternoon," makes it difficult for Billy to believe both statements: "I love you...," - "I'm going to put you out..."

Except when the clear meaning of an observation depends on a statement of absolute exception, "and" can be used in the place of "but" in our communication transactions. "And" causes less defense-reaction, helps us handle our own defensive feelings, directs our attention to our true intentions and makes our connected-clause sentences make sense. Whenever possible, scratch your "but" and use "and" and your communication will be more effective.

Consider again the scene with the mother and the little boy. She wants him to stop slamming the door. Whether he does or not may well depend on what goes on inside his psyche when he feels unloved and defensive. "Billy, I love you, AND if you slam that door one more time I'm going to put you out in the back yard and keep you there all afternoon." The "and" brings both clauses together and makes them both believable. The "and" gives Billy a better chance of handling his defensive feelings in a constructive way.

SEVEN-STEP PROCESS FOR CHANGE

THE process for changing or for getting well, done individually, one-on-one or in groups, is a movement from an awareness of the problem to an awareness of alternatives and a decision. I see it as a series of seven questions (the last one as a review of the first six,) all of which are responded to by the individual desiring change (rather than by the therapist or by some other person.)

1. Where do I hurt?
2. How would I like the situation to be different?
3. What have I done about the problem so far?
4. What gains do I get out of keeping things as they are?
5. What alternatives do I have?
6. What do I plan to do?
7. How can I sabotage my plan?

In any situation where change is desired an understanding of this process can be productive. The steps that take place in successful change are not always in the well-defined order given here but the movement tends to be from number "1" through number "6". Step number "7" is frequently not considered although its inclusion sheds light on what has happened in the past to cause failure and provides some cognitive guarantee of success for present decisions.

This process for change can be used in changing the self, in helping others to change and in changing organizational process or structure. When working with others, "she," "he," or "they" may be substituted for "I" wherever "I" occurs. In working with organizations, any of the above pronouns may be pertinent and/or "the organization" may also be used, i.e. "Where does the organization hurt?" etc. The following considerations are important.

Step #1 implies that wherever change is sought it is because there is an awareness of discomfort or hurt. It is sometimes easier to uncover the hurt by going to step #2 and thinking in terms of how the individual or organization would like things to be instead of the way things are.

Step #3 carries an implication that what has been tried thus far has failed. Be aware that that may not be due to a lack of validity in what was tried and that, in fact, what has been tried in the past may be worthy of using again.

Step #4 probes at the reasons for failure in making the desired changes. We tend to keep things as they are for five reasons:

- to avoid being aware of our inward feeling,
- to avoid facing a frightening outward circumstance,
- to avoid changing the way we structure our time,
- to avoid changing our basic position toward ourselves and others,
- to avoid losing the strokes (probably negative strokes) we have become accustomed to getting for behaving in our present way.

In step #5 and step #6 it is important to allow the individual concerned to come up with the alternatives and the plan to be implemented. To do otherwise is to deny the autonomy that is essential to successful change.

Step #7 enables one to discover how and why past attempts at change have failed. Coupled with step #4 this step brings an awareness of those repetitive behavior patterns that are destructive to the changes wanted in a life or an organization. Being aware of the desired changes and the patterns that have kept them from being realized brings a powerful motivation to change.

THE INTERPRETATION OF DREAMS

My schematic for interpreting dreams relies on Sigmund Freud's basic understanding of the structure and function of dream work, the Gestalt method of telling the dream in the first person present and owning each part of it plus interpreting the evolution of feelings that runs through the dream and the linkage of those feelings with an early significant memory. It holds to the idea that most of an individual's dreams consistently express the same core life-problem, i.e. the unconscious struggle of that individual with the most significant dilemma of his life.

Freud called dreams "the royal road to the unconscious" and as late as 1931 he wrote in a forward to Brill's translation of *The Interpretation of Dreams*: "(This work) contains...the most valuable of all the discoveries it has been my good fortune to make." He distinguished between the terms "latent dream," "manifest dream" and "dream work" and reserved the term, "dream" to designate the total phenomena of which the first three terms are component parts. The "meaning of a dream" signifies the latent dream content as it comes mainly from the unconscious and also from the area of current concerns.

THE LATENT DREAM

The latent dream content is made up of three component parts:

- Sensory impression, e.g. the discomfort of cold or heat, the sound of a siren, urinary urgency,
- Thoughts and feelings associated with current concerns, e.g. worry over a loan payment or the preparation of a speech; anxiety about the safety of one's children, the hope of a happy event in the future and,
- Impulses from the repressed unconscious mind, essentially of childhood.

While not always are all three of these components present, in almost all dreams the third one is essential. Freud believed that the essential part of the latent dream content always comes from the repressed unconscious mind and that without it there would be no dream. It also seems to be true that there are usually elements of current waking concerns present in the latent dream.

THE MANIFEST DREAM

The manifest dream is that which is experienced by the dreamer which he may or may not recall and talk about in his waking state. In the Gestalt method of dream interpretation the manifest dream is the dreamer, i.e. the person dreaming is the creator of all the elements of the dream so that all elements are parts of him. Thus, in a dream where I am walking through a forest where there are birds singing and I come out of the forest onto a sandy beach with the ocean surf lapping at my feet and several strangers engaged in playing volleyball who ignore me, I am the forest, I am the birds, I am the beach, I am the ocean surf, I am the several strangers, I am the volleyball game, I am even the volleyball!

The furniture of the dream often comes partly from the dreamer's experiences of the last 24 hours and it is worthwhile to recognize that fact in the interpretation as a linkage to other associations. So, in the above dream I may have driven by a group playing volleyball in a park, and I may have noticed the singing of birds as I raked my lawn.

The Dream Work

The function of a dream is to preserve sleep, to keep us from waking. To do this the latent dream must be translated into something not too objectionable. Freud's three dreamwork factors come into play.

The first of these factors is Freud's assertion that dreaming is a process of gratifying an id impulse, in essence a **wish fulfillment**, a feature that he never succeeded in explaining satisfactorily. My own explanation is that it is wish fulfillment in that it attempts to solve the core dilemma of a life, the central problem with which the ego has struggled in hope of resolution. That would be true wish fulfillment, the wish that the central problem of my life (with which I am probably not in touch) be solved. I think this is what Freud sensed but never understood in speaking of dreams as wish fulfillment. In my own life I know the core problem. It is the driving need to be authentic. That means that when I speak I want it to come from the real me, adequately thought through and carefully decided and prepared. It also means that I often feel unauthentic, that I receive honors without earning them. While my dreams are usually pleasant they all reflect this struggle. I dream that I am about to speak to an audience and I am unprepared. In one dream I stand at the bottom of a curved stairway and a steady stream of beautiful girls descend, each one giving me a kiss. Remember, I am also the girls and as I take on their image I wonder if I really mean that kiss!

The second factor is the operation of the defenses of the ego, which Freud called, **the dream censor**, and which is concerned with the continued suppression of the repressed latent dream impulse and the prevention of its appearance in the conscious manifest dream. It also tries to bar from appearance the unpleasant current concerns. The censor cannot prevent these unpleasurable impulses and concerns from forcing their way into our manifest dream but it can and does disguise and distort the elements so that they are unintelligible.

So, Sharon, a navy wife, is concerned about her husband's absence in Japan, afraid that he might have a sexual affair with a Japanese woman while he's away from home as her father did with a woman when she was five years old. She dreams not that Ronald is absent but that her car remains overnight in the driveway and that it is stolen, not by a Japanese woman but by a Spanish-American man. In this dream the husband is disguised as her car, (in telling the dream she said that the car Remained Over Night in the driveway, an odd way of saying that she left the car in the driveway all night, but notice that the first letters of each word spell, RON, which is what she called her husband) and her guilt about her treatment of him is disguised as *leaving the car out over night.* Her fear of losing him to a Japanese woman is distorted to make it appear that a Spanish-American man is stealing the car.

By way of disguise and distortion things that appear together in the latent dream content may appear far apart in the manifest dream, emotions may appear transformed from positive to negative or vice-versa, Vagueness may indicate a strong censorship. Freud used the term "compromise" to indicate such alterations of content. In dream interpretation it is important to look closely at such compromises. Negative awarenesses, e.g., the dreamer reports that she "did not feel sexual," or "did not feel afraid," probably should be interpreted as feeling sexual and feeling afraid. Reversals, such as a man reporting that, in the dream, he is a woman, need to be noted. Displacement. the attachment of an affect to something other than its proper object, polarities of contrasting objects, and omissions, as well as odd word formations and slips of the tongue in reporting the manifest dream, all bear close scrutiny.

The third factor, Freud called **secondary elaboration**. By this he meant the attempt on the part of the ego to form the otherwise unintelligible dream into a semblance of logical coherence. The ego attempts to shape the distorted dreamwork into something that makes enough sense to the dreamer so that he won't awaken. This factor helps to shape the final form of the manifest dream. It contributes to the distortion and disguise.

THE METHOD OF INTERPRETATION

In the interpretation of a dream it is important that the dreamer draw his own conclusions as to meanings, the therapist acting only as a guide. She asks questions in order to clarify rather than making suggestions about what an item of the manifest dream might represent. The sequence of the interpretation is as follows:

1. **Have the dreamer tell the manifest dream as he remembers it.** Accept all impressions recounted including feelings of tentativeness where the dreamer says, "I'm not sure that I dreamed it this way but it seems like it." As the dreamer relates the dream, list the feelings that accompanied the dream in the order they are related. I use a blank page with a line drawn down the middle. On the left side I list the main furniture of the dream. On the right side I list everything that can be interpreted as a feeling.

For example, this afternoon, during a nap I had this dream:

I dreamed that I was in a huge lecture hall where I had to make a presentation. People were assembled. I was behind the scenes with another speaker who was to follow me. He was busy with his notes. I was doing nothing to get ready except being nervous. I looked at our notes. They were slabs of thin gristle with very little meat. The gristle must be opened up to get to the meaning of what I wanted

to say. I asked the other speaker, "Who presents today,
you or I?" He said, "I think you do." I figured I would
muddle through.

The main furniture of the dream is:
- Huge lecture hall
- "Assembled" people
- Backstage
- Other speaker
- Notes as "slabs" of thin gristle
- Very little meat

The feeling content is:
- Having to...
- Being" assembled (dissembling)
- Being behind
- Following
- Being busy and doing nothing
- Feeling very little
- Must (having to)
- Wanting to
- Feeling of inquiring, "who?"
- Feeling of thinking
- Feeling of figuring
- Feeling of muddling through

2. Talk about the furniture of the dream. Bring out
any connection with experiences within the past twenty-four
hours.
  Three things occur to me:
- The hall looks like a church. Today is Sunday and I felt
  like I should go to church today.
- I went to the grocery today and considered buying a
  slab of pork ribs.

- I received a fax yesterday reminding me that I am to meet with an organization to do team-building.

Here is represented my extreme moral and Welsh up-bringing, my sense of duty and of doing things "right." Here also, is represented my selfish side; I love pork ribs, fat, gristle and all, even though I know about cholesterol. And here is represented my anxiety about being prepared to team-build: an atmosphere of trust must be established and authenticity is the "meat" of trust.

3. Ask the dreamer to recall an early memory. Record the feelings that accompany the events of the memory. My early memory is of being a nine-year-old with scarlet fever. It is Thanksgiving day, the family is gathered in the dining room except for me. I am bed-ridden and have been told to eat no solid food. While the family is at the table I get up, steal into the kitchen and eat some turkey. My feelings are guilt for not following the strict rules and fear that something terrible will happen for doing something forbidden.

4. Ask the dreamer to repeat the dream, this time in the present tense, owning each part of it. I am in a huge lecture hall part of me where I have to make a presentation part of me. The people part of me are assembled. I am in the (back-stage) part of me with another speaker part of me who is to follow me. The other speaker part of me is busy with his notes part of me. I am doing nothing but being nervous. I look at our notes part of me. They are slabs of thin gristle part of me with very little meat part of me. The gristle part of me must be opened to get to the meaning part of me. I ask the other speaker part of me, Who presents today, the you part of me or the I part of me?" The other speaker part of me says, "I think you do" I figure I will muddle through.

5. Ask the dreamer to state what comes to mind as he thinks about the dream. I am thinking about how often in life I seem to be the subject of good fortune or of someone's goodwill instead of being adequately prepared for the task I performed. I am thinking of how so many good things have come my way unearned. And I am thinking of a friend's suggestion to me: "You deserve anything you can afford."

6. **Point out the evolution of feelings within the dream and within the early memory and ask for the dreamer to speak about any relationships or patterns they bring to mind.** The evolution of feelings within the dream were: Having to, Being assembled (I associate the word as a displacement for the word "dissemble" which means "to put on a false appearance,"); Being behind, Following and Being busy doing nothing all seem to mean that I spend my time "spinning my wheels" and depending on others; Feeling little speaks to the resulting image of low self-worth; Having to and Wanting to speak to the polarity within me which wants to be authentic; Feeling of Inquiring, "who," means the search for an identity; Feeling of Thinking and of figuring, indicates a duplicity within me that seeks to manipulate and the Feeling of Muddling through, means that I can relax, I will "make it" after all.

The evolution of feelings within the early memory speaks to the same inward doubts, fears and hopes.

7. **Point out anomalies such as repetition and repetitive patterns, slips of the tongue, omissions and changes in the second telling of the dream, polarities within the dream, vagueness, negative awareness and strange wordings. Ask the dreamer to relate to those things.** I have already mentioned the strange wording "assembled" in the dream above. My association to it was "dissembled" which is the key to the meaning of my dream. A polarity in the dream has also been mentioned, a sense of duty and wanting to be authentic diametrically opposed to my behavior in the dream of "doing nothing but being nervous."

8. It is sometimes useful to ask the dreamer to assume the identity of a furnishing of the manifest dream, e.g. to be the slab of thin gristle: and in that identity and in the first person present speak of what it is like to be that object.

I am the slab of thin gristle. I have very little of substance, but I can be opened up to reveal meat and meaning. And I can sustain life if I am used properly.

TED'S DREAM

I am alone in a cabin in the wilderness. It is an open space. I see a humming bird and suddenly I am struck by a bee or a hornet that chases me until I squash it. Suddenly I am struggling with a woman. I am straddling her but I am impotent. It turns out that she is a diabetic woman who will not take her insulin. I am trying to convince her to take the needle and she is OK.

The furniture of the dream:
- Wilderness cabin
- Open space
- Humming bird
- Bee/hornet
- Woman
- Needle

The feeling content is:
- Feeling open
- Feeling struck
- Feeling chased (chaste?)
- Feeling squashed
- Feeling straddled (noncommitted?)
- Feeling not taken
- Feeling convinced

- Feeling forced
- Feeling OK

Ted immediately associated the hornet sting with the current concern and the furniture of having his blood pressure taken the day before.

Ted's early memory at the age of nine is of being given an inspection for pin worms by his father and then being given an enema. In recalling this experience he recalled the accompanying feelings. He felt exposed and invaded.

From his interpretation of the dream Ted recognized his core life-problem as one of sexual identification. He had felt forced by his father into an open inspection of his anal region and wondered if he had had a homosexual experience with the insertion of the enema tube. His next association was to his mother's demand that he not touch his penis: that he remain "chaste." He was slapped by his father when he did not stand up for himself in a childhood fight: "I felt like a little girl." In short, Ted felt a life-long anxiety about being exposed (open to others) as a homosexual. At this point in his therapy Ted was used to *permissions* and *protections* and that is the source of the "feeling OK.," meaning "Its OK to have my blood pressure taken and have it in a normal range." and "Its OK to have an identity problem and still be masculine." In this sense it was what I call a *putting together* dream.

There are many other factors in the dream capable of interpretation, such as the polarity between the humming bird and the hornet, and the interpretation of the word, "chased" or "chaste." I could have had Ted assume the identity of the humming bird and, in the first person present, tell what it is like to be the humming bird. *I am pretty. I am small and fragile.* Then I could have had him assume the identity of the hornet. *I am fierce and I have a stinger.* But we have already demonstrated the method of interpreting dreams.

Notice that in the interpretation some, even most, of the lists of furniture and the feelings go un-noticed and uninterpreted. Nevertheless the therapist lists the main furniture and the main feelings because she does not know which pieces of furniture and which feelings will be most important to the dreamer.

CHILDHOOD DREAMS, NIGHTMARES AND OTHER ANXIETY DREAMS

In this chapter on dream interpretation there has probably arisen a question about the dream censor in that in certain dreams there seems to be a direct translation of the elements (dreams of early childhood) or a lack of suppression of the frightening elements as in nightmares and punishment dreams.

Childhood dreams can be explained by the lack of systematized repression in early childhood, allowing things to appear in the dream almost as they are in reality. So Ted, dreaming of the threat of surgery on his penis, needed little interpretation to understand that his penis represented a threat to him. A child may dream of finding something she has lost, or of going to a circus after seeing the advertisement on television. Such dreams appear to be direct translations of the elements in the dream.

For nightmare and anxiety dreams the only plausible explanation is that the censor fails to bar the frightening material from the manifest dream. In punishment dreams, where one dreams of being punished, the explanation is probably that the ego anticipates guilt if the repressed material is allowed to enter into the manifest dream, bars the material, and entertains the guilt for which punishment is felt to be deserved.

Dream interpretation, when done according to this schematic, can be an important adjunct to therapy in that it uncovers the core problem of one's life along with the fear and anger and wish that accompany it. In this chapter we have presented a plan for interpreting dreams based on Freud's structure and function of dream work and the Gestalt method of owning each part of the dream as part of oneself. To that we have added what I consider to be the most rewarding feature of dream interpretation: the evolution of feeling patterns revealed in the telling of the dream and the linkage of those feelings with an early significant memory. In this part of the interpretation one comes face to face with the core life-problem and the struggle to come to terms with it.

FINDING MEANING IN LIFE

THERE are six things that give meaning to life, that make me want to live rather than die. They are: basic survival, obsessions, relationship, anticipation, service, and diet and exercise.

• Basic Survival. When I am engaged in that fundamental struggle, life seems precious in contrast to its alternative: death. Philip Wylie tells somewhere about visiting London at the height of the German blitzkrieg when the lives of everyone hung in the balance and nightly air raids were being sustained with a tremendous loss of life and property. He expected the people of London to be downcast, depressed and gloomy. Instead, he found them exuberant, alert and living with a sense of humor. He said of them, "They were living at their highest level." Involved in a struggle to survive, life took on new and deep meanings for those Londoners.

• Obsession. To be obsessed with some challenge gives meaning to life. That's the part that goals play in our lives. Show me a person who has no goals and I'll show you a despairing person, for whom life has little or no meaning. Obsessions are fueled by a combination of fear and hope and it is the hope part of the fuel that gives life its greater meaning. The obsession may be "magnificent," concerned with lofty ideals such as the development of a preventive vaccine for AIDS, or it may be more mundane: the procurement of something, a car, a home, a new pair of shoes. Or it may be the pursuit of relationship. Always, hope is involved, along with the feared effect on me if I don't achieve my obsession.

• Relationship. There are five sets of relationship that import meaning into my life. They are play, work, bitching, taking care of, and being taken care of. When Karl Menninger was asked for a definition of mental health, he replied, "A mixture of work, play and love in one's life." Later when he was asked what he would do if he felt he were having an emotional breakdown, he said, "I would immediately find somebody who needs help and help him." My definition of mental health involves all four of these things that Dr. Menninger mentioned, plus two more: bitching and being taken care of, and involves all of them as a part of relationship. In my relationships do I have someone to play with, someone to work with, somebody who will hear my complaining and may complain back to me, someone to take care of and someone to take care of me? If you find life not worth living, look at these sets of relationships and see where you are lacking. A full, meaningful life includes them all.

• Anticipation. Hope is always concerned with the future. Hope is a function of relationship so that when it is lacking, look for a fracture of relationship. To anticipate achievement in the realm of survival, obsession or relationships is a key to finding meaning in life. Always have in mind something to anticipate: a visit from someone, the beginning of a class, the coming of a season, the cleaning of the house, giving a bath to the dog or cat, the start of a new job, or even going to bed at night and getting up in the morning.

• Service. Service is a part of relationship. But here I have in mind doing something for somebody for which you receive no remuneration, perhaps not even a "thank you." This is what Karl Menninger had in mind when he said he would begin helping somebody. Focusing my attention on myself is focusing on the area where misery is found. Happiness, on the other hand is always felt at the periphery of situations. So, when I ask Sally, stooped over a washing machine where she is doing the laundry for four kids, "Are you happy," she has to stop and think for a moment before she answers, "Yes, I think I am." Misery is always found at the center of my attention. To focus on someone outside of myself is a key to finding meaning in life. This is especially true when by decision we help someone near or far away and accept the ego-satisfaction that comes with the knowledge that, "I have served."

• Diet and Exercise. To participate in obsession, relationships, anticipation and service we must have energy, and energy comes from proper diet and exercise. Proper nutrition is almost always neglected. It involves listening to my own body and following its requests and it also calls for some training in nutrition. Exercise can be defined in terms of aerobics: the providing of oxygen to the body cells. That means something like twenty to thirty minutes of continuous exercise at least three or four times a week with the heart rate elevated to a meaningful tempo. There are several methods for arriving at the meaningful heart-rate level. (One is the "Karvonen Equation:" 220, minus your age, minus your resting heart rate, times 0.7, plus your resting heart rate equals your Target Heart Rate.) A proper amount of exercise often defeats depression, usually overcomes malaise and adds energy for living.

What I Believe About Decisions

"Decisions: The act or process of deciding."

"Decide: To arrive at a solution that ends uncertainty or dispute about."

-Webster's Ninth New Collegiate Dictionary

THE long-range goal of therapy is the achievement of autonomy, the governing of the self by the self. I speak of this as TCOL, Taking Charge of my Own Life. The instrument for that is decision-making. I take charge of my own life by making decisions about my behavior. I differentiate between "decision" and "choice." For me, "choice" implies a feeling-process that may or may not involve thoughtful selection, from a somewhat narrow range of options. "Decision" implies a thinking process that includes feeling, and a much wider range of alternatives. The word, "decision," can also be used in an adjectival, descriptive, form, "decisive," which graphically portrays a process of thoughtful determination.

The startling and beautiful discovery that I am in charge of my own life does not discount the effect that genes and environment and trauma have had on my life course or present situation. It is simply to discover that, given the parameters of my personal world, I am still in charge: I carry the responsibility for where I am, what I do, and the direction in which I am moving.

To assume this responsibility I must make decisions. So what is involved in making a decision? There are nine things that I have come to believe about decision making:

1. Decision making takes very little time: it is the reluctance to make decisions that takes so much of our time.

2. The reason we take so much time with not making decisions is that we believe there is always the right decision and any other decision is wrong. It is true, of course, that when you go in one direction you forego another direction.

3. All decisions are made with insufficient evidence. If there is sufficient evidence we don't have to make a decision; we know which button to push.

4. If evidence is considered inadequate, and time allows, a decision can be made to postpone a decision on the matter at hand.

5. The most important aspect of decision-making is not what we decide but the act of deciding, the assertion of my right to take charge of my own life.

6. The second most important aspect of decision-making is what I do with the consequences resulting from the decision: what I do with the decision after I have made it.

7. When I make a decision I know the reason for it. I may also be able to garner one or more justifications to support it, but there is one over-riding reason for the decisive act. Justifications may be useful, but they do not indicate that a decision has been made.

8. When I make a decision, I do not feel guilty about it. I may feel sadness or grief, but I do not carry that haunting sense of unworthiness that characterizes guilt.

9. Any decision can be re-decided. a decision is not a commitment. The word "commitment" smacks of the irrevocable. A decision is always negotiable. A decision is an opportunity for investment of energy. If and when the evidence warrants I can re-decide where I will invest my energy. If I decide to get married I can decide to break the engagement or later, to get unmarried. Re-deciding does not give me immunity from the consequences of a previous decision. I can decide to take a plane from Washington to New York. While passing over Philadelphia I can re-decide to go to Los Angeles. I will still have to land in New York before carrying out my re-decision.

Most of us live our lives without making many, if any, decisions. Some people live on the basis of rights and wrongs: doing what is "right" and avoiding what is "wrong." Or they live according to the way life is supposed to be lived, doing what they should do. These people may grow up, get married, have children, buy cars, buy a home, perhaps have a heart attack and die, without making decisions about any of those major events. Other people live on the basis of what they want, doing what they want and avoiding what they don't want. They too go through the major events of their lives without decisions. The people who live by the "shoulds" may be successful but they have little joy in their lives. The people who live by their "wants" have few meaningful relationships.

Autonomy means that I hold decisive power in my own life. If you want to begin experiencing making decisions, the way to do it is to practice on little things: deciding what I will wear today, what I will eat this morning, what I will do with my free time this weekend. Make it a conscious process. Don't make it a complicated procedure: just elevate your consideration of alternatives into your conscious awareness and on the basis of present evidence, select one of them and give the reason, e.g., "I decide to get to work by nine o'clock this morning." Reason: "I want to keep my job."

THE GAME OF ROMANTIC LOVE

THE loss of a romantic love object to another person produces a pain that is almost impossible to communicate. The pain produces jealousy and is often manifested in bizarre behavior. Although what I am going to say about it will not stop the pain, it can lead to a clear understanding of the pain and provide a basis for getting through it.

• It's OK to hurt! That's a beginning. Very few people make it through life without experiencing that kind of pain, and in a way, those few are the ones to be pitied because they have missed an experience that enriches life and expands one's awareness and understanding of other lives. To love is to hurt or at least to risk hurt. In any love-situation that continues past the first romantic stage there is always an imbalance of feelings, i.e., one person Needs the other more than the other needs him/her. That imbalance can shift, and usually does, from time to time with the heavy Need moving from one person to the other, but the amount of need/need is almost never a 50/50 situation. One person has the "leg up" or power position in the relationship at any given time.

For example, here's a man whose relationship with a woman, Mary, has more often than not been one of her Needing him more than his needing her. He told her when he went away on a solo trip that he felt it important not to have a committed, exclusive relationship. At that point she felt the hurt; he had the "leg up" position. His need for her did not become heavy at all until he began to sense that she was changing in some way; needing him less. That is the story of romantic love as it is played day by day throughout the Western World.

In a way it's a game, romantic love. The goal is to re-inforce my identity as a potent male or female person. I am most comfortable when I perceive the other person needs me. Then I may become complacent and a little bored. The other person, alarmed, begins to pressure me and, in reaction to that pressure I pull away a little more. Eventually, the other person, by decision or from exhaustion, lets loose of me and includes a new person into his/her life. Now I, sensing that I have lost my power position, become alarmed and try to re-form the relationship. If it appears doubtful I become jealous and start applying pressure, but the other person now feels the sense of potency, the "leg up" position, and is reluctant to give it up.

The hurt, which is felt so terribly, is actually a crushed Ego. I doubt that there is anything more painful. The feeling is one of being unable to do anything to change the situation. It is a beating of my wings against blackness. I lose appetite, become sleepless, find music difficult to listen to and altogether lose my sense that life has meaning.

So what can you do when you feel that despair? You can first know that it's OK to hurt, that the hurt is the pain of a crushed Ego and that it is not fatal unless you allow it to be.

• Second, you can non-attach (see the diagram). Non-attachment is not detachment. I can still let the other person know I care, BUT I do not pressure in any way. Non-attachment is an intellectual decision that my life is not dependent upon the other person: that whatever he/she does I can live and be and enjoy my life. At the feeling level I still hurt. At the thinking level I know that I can get on with my own life and, that whatever he/she does, it is imperative that I discover that my living and being and enjoying cannot be dependent upon him/her. If the other person then decides to re-form the relationship it will be because he/she sees that I can get on with my life. If he/she does not decide to re-form the relationship it is even more important that I have taken care of myself, independently, by non-attaching.

The Significant Other's Life-->

_____

Your Life -->

_____

NON ATTACHMENT

Notice that non-attachment differs from detachment in that I allow myself to accept invitations to closeness from the other person and can issue invitations to closeness to him/her. I assume the power position of deciding when to do either of these actions. If in the acceptance or issuing of invitations I find that I suffer more than I want to suffer, I can decide to withhold these actions.

• Third, you can keep busy. This means structuring your time so that you do not have time for withdrawal and analysis of what might have been or what was. You have enough structure that you don't spend time looking for evidence that he/she does or does not care. It means that by Wednesday morning of each week, you have your week-end planned, not waiting to see if by some sudden change he/she will become a part of it. It means that you have other things filling your hours so that you do not have time to write or telephone your desperate Need to him/her.

• Fourth, you can open your life to invitations of friendship from other people. It is true that there are hundreds of thousand of men and women out there with whom I can form a healthy, happy relationship and someday, when I'm not searching through field glasses I'll see him/her. In the meantime I can appreciate touching the lives and thoughts and feelings of other people and allowing them to touch my life and thoughts and feelings.

• Fifth, you can get plenty of exercise, letting the sadness motivate the kind of exercise that produces energy and a feeling of well-being.

• Sixth, you can allow your hurt to escalate into anger, i.e., resentment and/or defiance. Decide to be angry and you'll hurt a little less.

• Seventh, you can take advantage of this opportunity to relieve your crushed Ego a bit by deciding to summon your energy to stop a behavior that you have long wanted to stop, (smoking, over-indulgence in food or drink), or to start an activity that you have often thought of doing, (taking up skiing or skating or writing, or reading). Taking such positive action adds to your self-esteem and allows you to feel better about yourself.

None of this indicates a cynicism about love. Romantic love is a game, and no one of us escapes playing it. Beginning with that, love can develop into an affection that is free of ego-hurt or almost free of it. But love usually begins with romantic love and it is the normal fate of man and woman to feel the hurt that you are feeling.

Nor is any of this a magic potion to stop the hurt. It is only a way to endure it and to gain the best from it.

It is well that another person cannot take away the hurt because that would cause the hurting one to miss the vital, human experience, an experience which will, if you allow it, someday prove to be a friend.

DEMAND

EACH of us grows up with an image that we and the world are supposed to fit. When the world or someone in it doesn't fit the image I feel like I have been let down and I may feel despair. If, at that point, I demand that the world or the person change, I am headed for disappointment. The way out of that might be to give myself permission to accept a world that is not the way I want it to be.

When I don't fit the image I have superimposed upon myself I feel that, in some way, I am not real, or not authentic. I think the essence of that feeling is a voice inside that says, "You ain't like other people!" If, at that point, I demand that I change I am bound to be disappointed. The way out of that might be to give myself permission to be a unique person, with all of the "different" feelings and thoughts and behaviors that I have.

It has been helpful to me to get rid of demanding changes in myself and other people. That doesn't mean giving up hoping and expecting and even praying that I and others will change. It's part of health to hope and expect and pray that my aspirations will be actualized. I can even work for change. But to demand change in myself or others is to be disappointed.

I recognize the struggle this sets up in my psyche: the struggle between my aspirations and the world of real. I have been there and am perhaps still there with one difference.

Somewhere along the path I stopped fighting the realities in myself, in others and in the world that I cannot change. I still have hope and I expect and work for change, but most of the demanding I have given up. And, to my surprise, sometimes I discover that in the struggle with my discontent I have been enriched far beyond those who do not struggle.

THE DEMAND LADDER

WHEN you feel threatened you feel defensive, and a defensive feeling is a sign of anger. If you wonder about that statement it is probably because of an old prejudice against feeling anger: that anger is intrinsically bad when, in fact, it is a natural and normal preparation of a being to protect itself when afraid.

A major trigger for defensive feeling is the hearing or sensing of any demand. It may be universal to feel resistance when confronted by demand. A high percentage of people resist even a mild suggestion because of the fear of being controlled.

Since defensive behavior tends to defeat communication we are more effective communicators when we reduce demand to a minimum level. Of course, when communication is flowing smoothly there is no requirement to follow any rules. When communication is breaking down, stagnating or has reached an impasse one principle to remember is, reduce the demand.

The Demand Ladder shows how demand increases as we move from owning our own feeling, through passive manipulation, to critical judgment:

•__/ Why don't you? (most demand)....__/
•__/ You should............................__/
•__/ I need................................__/
•__/ I wish................................__/
•__/ I want................................__/
•_/ I'd like (least demand)........__/

An "I'd like" is an expression of one's own feeling and carries no demand. Just as we are entitled to any feeling that we have, we are entitled to any "I'd like" in the world, and for the same reason: because we cannot be rid of it by willing it away. "I'd likes" are specific statements of feeling and like feelings they do change from time to time but not by any act of dispossession. If we are going to relate with other people it becomes our right and our responsibility to decide what "I'd likes" to reveal to them. To relate to another person I need to know something about where that other person is in terms of his/her feelings and "I'd likes."

An "I want" carries a little more demand. The demand is signaled in the semantics: to "want" is to be lacking in something.

"I wish" expresses a yearning that is hard to resist without feeling guilty. It is passively manipulative with a hint of dishonesty in its pressure on the other person to fulfill my wish.

"I need" is almost always an untruth in normal conversation. Needs are bottom-line items--requirements for the maintenance of self-worth and/or health. To express a "need" is to invite the other person to feel bad if he/she does not meet the need. Many participants in training courses for self-assertiveness begin to use the words, "I need..." as a way of asserting selfness. Usually it is perceived by the other person as a manipulative ploy with heavy demand and defended against with resistance.

"You should (ought to)" transfers the emphasis from the "I" to the "you" and carries with it a critical judgment which almost always raises defensive feelings and defensive behavior.

"Why don't you...?" communicates the heaviest demand of all. Consider what it means when translated clearly: "Justify, if you can, why you do not take the action that I suggest to you." It is a demand for justification of one's behavior, or one's thinking or one's feeling. Most people use "Why don't you....?"

as a soft way of making a suggestion when, in reality, it contains more demand and triggers more defense than the other forms shown on the Demand Ladder.

Let's demonstrate the use of the Demand Ladder with two examples. First, a father speaking to his son about cleaning his room and, second, a man asking a woman-friend to have dinner with him.

1. Father, to son:
   - "I'd like you to clean your room." This statement carries no demand: it is a clear statement of where the father is in his feeling. (A feeling statement)
   - "I want you to clean your room." Demand is sensed in this statement: something is lacking. (Passive request)
   - "I wish you would clean your room." More demand: pressure is felt to meet the yearning. (Passive request)
   - "I need you to clean your room." "Need" indicates a bottom-line situation where something terrible will happen if "you" fail to meet my need. (Passive shift of responsibility)
   - "You should clean your room." Now the statement has moved from the simple-passive mode to the overtly judgmental. Judgmental pronouncements always trigger resistance. (Critical judgment)
   - "Why don't you clean your room?" This is a demand for an explanation of your attitude about room-cleaning and a justification of your behavior in the matter of room-cleaning. (Passive critical judgment) We are trained from childhood to think that it is "kind" to express judgments in a passive way rather than in a decisive way.

2.   Man, to woman-friend:
   - "I'd like you to have dinner with me."

- "I want you to have dinner with me."
- "I wish you would have dinner with me.
- "I need you to have dinner with me."
- "You should have dinner with me."
- "Why don't you have dinner with me?"

Ask any woman which of these statements would be most pleasing and elicit the least resistance and the most positive response.

It is important to remember that the principle of Demand-Resistance is not necessary when communication is flowing in a satisfactorily effective way. That is true of all principles of communication. Over-used they may get in the way. It is when you sense that communication is stagnating or breaking down or has reached an impasse that the rules become necessary.

It is also important to remember that all rules are suspended when time is of the essence, or it is a matter of life or death.

One further point needs to be made. there is a place in communication for demand. It is when the bottom line, or need-line has been reached and when other methods have failed. At such times when health, time, self-image or a required structure is at stake it may be necessary to demand. When it is necessary, demand should be made in a direct and decisive way, without superfluous words that dilute the message. For example, in the father-to-son illustration above, let's say that a prospective house-buyer is coming to see the house and it is time-important for the son to clean his room. The message is a clear demand message. "Clean your room!"

FOUR QUESTIONS

(TO ASK ONESELF ABOUT RELATIONSHIPS AND OWNERSHIPS)

EVERY relationship I have and every piece of equipment I own tends to complicate my life.

Friends and acquaintances and family members make demands on my time and energy. I have to be somewhere at a certain time, or relate to someone in a certain ways, so that my time is not as free as it would be without such accouterments. Even my dog and cat involve me in behaviors I would not have if I did not own them.

Since these people and things muddle my life it is well that I evaluate them in terms of costs and benefits. I can do that by answering four questions.

• What am I getting out of this relationship? What does the relationship do for me? What good things do I reap from having it? Do I get a sense of joy? A feeling of security? Companionship? This may be answered in terms of ego satisfactions as well as in terms of physical goods. So a mother feels good about taking care of a dependent child, and sad, but true, a wife may feel good about taking care of a dependent husband and a husband may enjoy the extra money that comes in from his working wife.

• What am I giving up in order to maintain this relationship? Every relationship requires me to give up something in order to maintain it. Being a father requires me to give up time that could be used in other ways. Being a parented child requires me to give up some freedoms. Being a friend calls for me to give up other friendships perhaps. Being a wife or husband may demand that I give up taking charge of my own life.

• How would I like the relationship to be? Getting in touch with how I'd like the relationship to be sets the automatic machinery to work to move the relationship in that direction. People who aren't in touch with how they would like things to be seldom arrive at the point where they have things the way they'd like them to be. People who know how they like relationships to be automatically move in that direction. Knowing what I'd like also helps in distinguishing my I'd likes from my requirements.

• What is my bottom line? What can I live with and what can't I live with and maintain my own health, dignity and self-worth? These are my requirements: the things I refuse to live with, or to live without. Many people maintain relationships for a lifetime and give up their health, their dignity and their sense of self-worth. For one who is determined to take charge of his/her own life, however, these are bottom lines and they are presented as such. They are, in a sense, presented as ultimatums, but they are not ultimatums. Thus, a wife who is unwilling to live with a passive husband would not say, "Unless you become decisive, I am going to leave," but would say instead, "I do not intend to continue to live with you in your passive ways."

These same questions may be asked with regard to the "things" I own. Every piece of equipment I own complicates my life by making demands on my time and energy. My clothes have to be laundered, my car has to be serviced, my tennis racket has to be placed somewhere when I've finished my game.

For example, my car. Answering these four questions:

1. I get transportation to work and play from it,
2. I give up a lot of money to own it,
3. I'd like it to be trustworthy and inexepensive.
4. I will not keep it if it breaks down frequently.

These four questions can help us evaluate whether we should decide to keep the relationships and the things which complicate our lives or decide to be rid of them. Answered honestly they can help us to accept the complications or to free ourselves of them.

Forgiving, Forgetting and Compassionate Understanding

I do not believe in forgiveness. The dictionary defines "forgive" as "Ceasing to feel resentment against (an offender)." That means I no longer demand that the situation be different from what it was. Demand is an internal stance and covered though it may be by time and circumstance, it can and does subtly raise its head when the pain of the original circumstance recurs.

I once was given a traffic ticket for passing through a red light. The light was green when I entered the junction but the driver of the car just ahead of me stopped and made an illegal right turn with my car underneath the light so that I could not see it. I resented the issuing officer and I resent him to this day when I think of the frequent injustices of traffic tickets. He could be my friend and I would still resent his behavior on that occasion.

Bring this down to where it hurts. Twenty years ago your four-year old child was run over and seriously injured by a drunk driver. Whenever you recall that incident you feel resentment for that driver. In order to erase the resentment you would have to forget that it happened.

We often couple the two words, "forgive" and "forget." That is correct in its image. To forgive is to forget. The old gospel hymn had it right, "Though my sins be as scarlet, they shall be as white as snow." In other words, the offense is no longer accountable; it is as though it had not occurred. It is forgotten! And since it is impossible to forget, it is impossible to forgive!

But there is a way to deal with the resentment so that it doesn't burn within us so much. Of course, time calluses over the sore spot to a degree. We "forget" that the incident occurred for hours, even days at a time. But depending upon the severity of the damage done, whenever we remember the "crime" we also remember the feeling of burning resentment.

The way to deal with that resentment is to come to a compassionate understanding of the person and the situation. If we remember that hostile and hurtful behavior is always a screen and a vehicle for fear-threat, it allows us to understand the workings of the police officer issuing the traffic ticket. Who knows what frustrations he had suffered on that particular day? If we take into consideration the fear forces that govern the drunken driver's drinking we can come to a compassionate understanding of his behavior. Why does anyone start to drink in the first place? Usually it's because of fear of ridicule by one's peers or the fear of rejection at a social gathering.

This principle becomes especially important in psychotherapy where so much blame for neuroses and psychoses, passivity and dependency, is deposited on our parents and their behavior toward us in our early years. We can't forgive them for their mistakes in rearing us if that means forgetting what they did. The memory is locked into our unconscious reactions to life. We can come to a compassionate understanding of those parents, on whom the forces of fear: fear of failing as a parent, fear of losing, fear of the loss of their selfness and fear of being cheated, played such a dramatic role.

In fact, someone has said that the end of successful psychotherapy is a compassionate understanding of one's parents. I believe that is true. And I would add to that, a compassionate understanding of other people and oneself.

One reason compassionate understanding is a more reasonable stance than forgiveness lies in the structural dynamics of each. Forgiveness, we have said, involves stopping a feeling of resentment and I believe that we never completely rid ourselves of any feeling. Compassionate understanding, on the other hand, is a cognitive behavior where one decides to accept the reason for the abuse. Understanding the reason allows us to have compassion on the abuser.

Not forgiveness, which involves forgetting, but an understanding which takes into account the forces that played upon and shaped the offending person, is the way to stop the burning sensation of resentment and free oneself to get on with one's own life.

That is the purpose of compassionate understanding. It eases the burden of resentment. It gets rid of hatred. It enables us to restore relationships with the offending person(s) if that is desirable, and in so doing removes one of the barriers we face in taking charge of our lives. As Nietzsche is reported to have said, "Nothing on earth consumes a man more quickly than the passion of resentment." And, "We can endure almost any 'how' if we know the 'why.'"

ANXIETY AND PANIC

Beneath every anxiety there is a "worst thing" fantasy. It can be unearthed by a series of questions including, "What is the worst thing than can happen to you when you are feeling that anxiety?" and "What is so bad about that for you?"

Lara, a thirty-six year old divorced woman had difficulty relating to men. She would get close to them, almost fall in love with them but at that point her anxiety would manifest itself and she would back away saying that she needed to be alone.

For four years she had had an on-again off-again relationship with a married man. After he moved out of his home and into an apartment she began to be quarrelsome with him, and absent herself from the relationship for several days at a time. When, at last he decided to detach from her and moved back into his home, Lara became very dependent on him, calling him at his office every day and resuming a daily sexual relationship with him.

At that point, the man moved out of his home again and promised Lara he would get a divorce. Almost immediately she withdrew from him, seeing him only for a few hours on Saturday afternoon and withdrawing sexually. When, finding the relationship to be too painful, he decided no longer to initiate rendezvous with her, she began calling him and suggesting dinner or an afternoon of bicycling or taking a long walk. During the course of these meetings she would begin with a warm greeting and then her anxiety would mount. She would turn noticeably cool, sometimes lagging behind him, becoming reticent and eventually ending the afternoon by initiating a quarrel, blaming him for trying to smother her. Finally she lied to him. She said that she didn't love him and that, in fact she was in love with an other man.

She came to me, stating that she knew that it was her problem, that he was an excellent companion and that she had engaged in the same contest with at least two other men in her past. She said, "When I get so close I get anxious."

Here is our conversation:

I: What is the worst thing that could happen if you commit yourself to a relationship with a man?

L: He will dominate me.

I: What's so bad about being dominated?

L: It will be like being imprisoned.

I: What's so bad about being imprisoned?

L: I wouldn't be able to do what I want to do and be what I want to be.

I: And what is so bad about that for you?

L: I'd feel cheated out of my birthright.

I: And what is so bad about losing your birthright?

L: It would be like I never ever existed. I just wouldn't be at all.

Lara's key underlying fear is not so much that she would lose control as she would be controlled. It is the basic fear of defiant people and is coupled with a usually conscious fear of being cheated. It is often expressed as the fear of "going down the drain." Lara felt that if she committed herself to a relationship with a man that she would cease to exist as a separate person.

Other basic fears are: the fear of losing, the fear of failing, and the fear of injustice. Each of them is fueled by the worst thing fantasy. They can be uncovered by pushing the questions, "What's the worst thing that can happen?" and "What's so bad about that.

Panic differs from anxiety in that it is attached to a single protocol in early childhood. That protocol carried the message, "Be careful!" meaning, "Something terrible is about to happen," Anxious parents give many "Be careful!" messages. But the person who has panic attacks can usually remember the single protocol that established the panic. It may be recalled by tracking back the panic feeling with the following suggestions and questions.

• Shut your eyes and get in touch with your panic. Where do you feel it in your body? Touch that part of your body (establishing the somatic counterpart of the feeling) Feel into those feelings and describe them.

• When have you had that feeling before? Speak in the first person present. (Accept any incident that comes to the subject's mind.) Describe the incident. What are the feelings that accompany it? (The feelings may be somewhat changed, but they will still be panic feelings. If the incident recounted is an early childhood incident go on to the next question. If it is more recent, repeat the present question.)

• What is the other person in the incident feeling? (This feeling will be a part of the panic feeling in the subject.)

• What are you feeling when this incident is going on? (This is also a part of the panic feeling.)

• What did you say inside your head at that time? (This is the trigger of the panic feeling that the subject has today. It usually has the flavor of "I'll show you...")

• What did you do? (This is the behavior that the subject engages in when he/she feels the panic. This behavior can be changed and when it is changed by re-decision, the feeling changes.)

Getting in touch with the protocol and deciding to change the behavior that accompanies the panic, reduces the panic feeling.

Sarah has panic attacks. She describes the feeling: "My chest feels tight. My heart pounds. I can't get my breath." I have her touch the area(s) of her body where she feels the panic.

I say, "Close your eyes. Tell me when you've had that feeling before."

Sarah: I'm five years old. My father and mother are arguing. I run to my mother. She picks me up. My father comes over and tears me out of her hands, puts me roughly on the floor and says, "Get away. Go to your room."

I: What is your father feeling?

Sarah: He is angry, he feels frustrated.

I: What is your mother feeling?

Sarah: She is scared. She yells at my father, "Be careful!"

I: What are you feeling?

Sarah: I am scared, I feel sick to my stomach. My mother is holding me tightly, I can't get my breath.

I: What did you say inside your head at that moment?

Sarah: I am thinking, this is the end of me.

I: What did you do?

Sarah: I didn't go to my room. I sat down in the corner of the room and watched them fight. ("I'll show you.")

I: How can you change your behavior now, instead of doing
   nothing and escalating your feeling of panic?

Sarah: I can control my own breathing and get on with whatever I am doing.

Sarah was following the protocol of her five-year-old experience. By deciding to change her behavior she controlled
her panic. This did not get rid of the frightening feeling, but it
made it powerless to control her feeling and her behavior.

How Do I Get Fired?

ONE of the most important things I can do in any situation is to figure out how to get fired. What are the limits beyond which I cannot go without getting consequences I don't want. When I know those limits, it is easier for me to be me and still stay within the box that is required. So long as I stay within the limits I can make my own decisions and take charge of my own life. Of course, I can decide to step outside the limits, if that is required for me to maintain my sense of worth and/or my health, and take the consequences of violating the limits.

Every life-situation constructs a box: the limits of which are fairly distinct. To move outside the box is to invite cultural anathema. The question I ask to establish what the limits are, is, "What is absolutely forbidden if I am to remain a welcomed participant in this structured relationship? in my family, my job, my church, my school, my country, my neighborhood, my other memberships and relationships?" And what must I do? For my job the bottom line may be that I get to work on time, dress appropriately, maintain a friendly countenance and accomplish a standard amount of the work-load. For my neighborhood the bottom line may be that I mow my yard regularly and keep the house in decent repair and not park any boats (or trailers or R.V.s) in the driveway. For my church it may be that I will be shunned if I get a divorce, or have an affair, or drink, or smoke or dance or play cards.

Once I know the limits I can decide whether I want to accept them and remain within the framework in good-standing, or step outside the framework and accept the consequences. If I step outside the box without deciding to do so, I will tend to blame the institution that rejects me. When I decide to "get fired" I accept full responsibility for my behavior.

The improvements in societal structures have probably come about because of decisions to move outside the box!

IDENTITY AND SELF-ESTEEM

Low self-esteem sometimes has its roots in an identity problem which bars self-acceptance. Central to my feelings of self-esteem is my sense of identity. There are at least two elements involved in my awareness that it is OK to be me.

One of these elements is my name. The other is my sexuality. Several studies have been made on the effect names have on people. Consider the influence on a young black man from Atlanta being called Martin Luther. And not many social case workers or missionaries have gone by the name of Trixie or Gigi.

My attention was first called to the importance of names by my own name, Harry David. In the village in which I was reared there was a feeble minded man, a close neighbor, whose name was Harry. Even as a child I understood the effect that name had on my sense of self-worth. I felt contaminated by the name and it was not by accident that years later I gladly accepted the change of being called by my initials, H. D. A frisky misuse of my name occurred at the age of twelve when a friend of my older brother, played with my full name, saying that he had to swear out a "harry david." (an affidavit.) This led me to understand that people do not like to have their names toyed with or misstated. I have watched the faces of men and women who have had their names mispronounced or punned and I am aware of their discomfort at such usage. My name is a key to my identity. To know that it is OK to be me, involves the fuller statement, "It is OK to be a person by the name of H. D."

The other element in one's identity consists of four crises that coincide with the development of the individual, all of which we pass through with a resolution that is more-or-less satisfactory. The last three of them involve our identity in terms of our sexuality.

• The first of these occurs between birth and about three months when the first awareness of my being different from "what's out there" takes place. The new-born infant probably has no sense of identity, but very quickly experience dictates that there is a difference between "me" and those entities who torment and frustrate me and nurture me. The resolution of this crisis is, "I am (more-or-less) a separate entity," "I am (more-or-less) an individual." The "moreness" or "lessness" is manifested in more symbiosis or less symbiosis, in more dependency or less dependency.

• The second identity crisis takes place probably between the second and third year of life. Until that time a little boy may consider being either a daddy or a mommy when he grows up. This crisis makes him aware that his possibilities are more limited than that. It is during this period that the child become aware that "I am (more- or-less) a boy," or "I am (more-or-less) a girl." Sexual identity is always a mixture of the feminine and the masculine. An individual who is one hundred percent masculine or one hundred percent feminine would be neither attractive nor interesting. Notice that we are not referring here to heterosexuality or homosexuality. I believe that is determined, for the most part, by genetic construct. We are referring to the masculine-feminine trait continuum that is present in both homosexuals and heterosexuals. Depending on how completely the resolution takes place, the boy takes on the identity of a boy, the girl of a girl, enhancing the identity or placing it in doubt.

• The third identity crisis takes place at puberty and

again it has to do with the individual's sexuality. It is during this period that the question of OKness becomes dominant. The resolution of this crisis results in "It is (more-or-less) OK to be a girl" or "It is more-or-less OK to be a boy." Given the disparity that has existed in opportunities for athletic competition and career pursuit at this stage of development, it is apparent that for many girls it does not seem OK to be a girl. Given the criticism rightly or wrongly heaped upon males in these past few decades, it is apparent that for many boys it does not seem OK to be a boy. Further, the boy may be confused about his sexuality if he has traits that are characteristically female traits, such as being gentle, and hearing and expressing feelings, or the girl, if she has characteristically male traits such as competitiveness and aggressiveness.

•   The fourth identity crisis begins with and follows on puberty. Here the crisis again has to do with OKness and sexuality. "It is (more-or-less) OK to be a grown-up boy," "It is (more-or-less) OK to be a grown-up girl." Being a grown-up boy or girl means that it is OK to marry and have children, to go to work and make a living, to take part in community life and to invest in the future.

So the second element in identity is three-fourths sexual. It seems to me that most people have some anxiety about their own sexuality. I have made that statement before thousands of people and have asked anyone present who has had no anxiety about his/her sexuality to speak to me about it. No one has yet come forward with that claim.

These two factors: my name and my sexuality are involved in my identity and therefore in my sense of self-esteem.

The solution to identity problems is the acceptance of one's self with whatever feelings one has and whatever handicaps one suffers. It is OK with me for me to be me and it is OK with me to feel anything I feel!

TEACHING

TEACHING, by word of mouth, in the meaning of giving instruction or advice, is only constructive when it is requested by the learner or when the situation is a matter of life or death, or when time is of the essence. There are two exceptions to this rule: in the rearing of children a parental figure must recognize that small children, according to their age, lack experience, e.g. in crossing streets, in table manners, in ordering their lives, in the values of the societal structure and need to be taught about such things. And school teachers, have an inherent privilege of teaching facts. Although the students have not specifically requested any given fact, their position as students indicates a tacit request to be taught.

The truth is that unless we request it, we human beings resent and resist being "taught." This is true of small children, who must be molded to fit into the various boxes in which every person lives. When my son, Douglas, was starting to play little league ball, he batted cross-handed. I tried to correct him and he defied me, saying that that was the way he wanted to bat. When his coach explained to him the advantage of placing his hands correctly on the bat, he accepted it readily. The difference was that he was a student and the coach had an inherent privilege of teaching him.

This speaks to the practice of friendship. Do not try to tell your friends what they should do unless they ask you for such information. It speaks to the practice of parenting older children. Do not, even gently, remind them of what they should do unless they ask for that kind of instruction. It speaks to the practice of counseling. It distinguishes counseling from coaching. A coach's task is to teach people, at their request, how to play games. A counselor's task is to enable people to take charge of their own lives. Occasionally a counselor is asked to give instruction or to answer a specific question. When that occurs he has entered a teaching mode at the request of the counselee. Until he receives such a request it is important that the counselor refrain from giving advice.

Teaching by example is different from teaching by precept. People tend to pattern themselves after models. Although being an example is subtle, it is powerful, far more powerful than giving advice. What we do speaks so loudly that others cannot hear what we are saying. This is especially true in the transmission of attitudes and attributes. You want your friend, your child, your patient to be truthful, trustworthy! then be that way with them. Tell them the truth and trust them. You want your son to be honest! then see to your own honesty. You want your daughter to take charge of her own life! then take charge of your own life!

When it comes to giving advice, don't do it. That, of course, is a piece of advice. So let me say it another way. Unless a person asks you for advice, it is important to refrain from giving it. And even when someone asks you for advice, it is important to explore with him his interest in the matter at hand. A person may ask me whether he should stay in his present job or move to a different one. My therapeutic response is, "You are interested in changing jobs, what would you like to do?" A danger in giving advice is that we do not know what another person should do. We are never smart enough to know another person better than she can know herself.

A second danger in giving advice is that should the advice prove destructive the recipient will blame you for it, should it prove constructive, he will give you all of the credit so that the next time he needs to make a decision, instead of deciding for himself, he will turn to another person for advice, and never reach the autonomous state of taking charge of his own life.

If I can't give advice;, what can I do? In situations where I am asked for advice the first response that comes to my mind is, "What would you like to do?" The second response that I think of is, "You are interested in (the situation mentioned or in making a decision about something.)" The third response that appeals to me is, "What alternatives do you have?" Along with these I might add, "Since you will bear the responsibility for what you do, I'd like you to come up with the possible solutions. All of these responses keep the ball in the home court of the person asking for advice and all of them indicate that I care about the individual asking for help. They remind the person that he is responsible for his own life and encourage him to take charge of it which is a primary goal of any therapeutic relationship.

In situations where I am tempted to teach without being asked, I resist giving advice. I am not my "brother's keeper," I should like to be his enabler. The first step in that process is "Do not teach anybody anything unless they ask to be taught!"

ANSWERING SERVICES

PROFESSIONAL graduate schools, while teaching a lot of practical theory and techniques, also teach their graduates what to do when they are confused about what to do. If we consider five professions: Law, Clergy, Social Case Work, Psychology and Medicine we will see how each provides an answering service to fall back upon when the professional person feels inadequate.

• Law. When the lawyer knows what his client should do, he explains the action in precise terms: fight, settle out of court, arbitrate or withdraw. When he is momentarily unsure of what to advise he brings in his "answering service." He asks the advisee to bring in a detailed listing of charges or claims or properties or behaviors that effect the action. This, while it may be useful, serves the purpose of stalling for time while the lawyer considers what advice to give..

• Clergy. When the minister has spent an hour with a parishioner and does not know what the problem being presented is, her "answering service" calls for prayer and meditation. Again, this may be useful in relieving a stressful situation, It also relieves the clergy person from finding out what the stressors are and advising the parishioner what might be done to relieve them.

• Social Case Work. The Social Case Worker-Therapist spends 50 minutes with a client who is being so general in her comments that the therapist cannot understand the specifics or being so specific in her statements that the therapist cannot grasp the bigger picture. Frustrated, the therapist calls on her "answering service," and begins taking a detailed "family history." The family history can provide insights into patterns of present behavior. It also provides the therapist with a sense that "I am doing something useful," and postpones the therapeutic process until a more advantageous time.

• Psychology. The Psychologist traditionally has been trained in psychological testing. That is her "answering service." When she is bewildered by the vagueness of her client, she automatically falls back on testing procedures. And while the Minnesota Multiphasic or the Meyer-Briggs or the Rorschach may provide clues to the personality problems of the client, they also delay the necessity for hearing and understanding and dealing with what is going on in the here-and-now.

• Medicine. The Medical Doctor is seen by most people as an absolute authority on physical ailments. When he sees an "ideal type" case of measles, he knows at once that it is measles. Often, however, diseases are not so ideal in their manifestations, leaving the physician in doubt as to exactly what he is seeing. So he goes to his "answering service": medication. "Take two of these with a glass of water and I'll see you again next week." The beauty of this is that if the medication is not effective at least the water will be good for the patient. If the medication is effective, (or the palliative or the placebo effect is positive), it is helpful. It is also helpful to the physician to stall for time until more evidence is presented or he can research what he has seen in Merck's Manual.

Most Professionals are motivated, at least in the beginning of their studies, by a genuine feeling of caring. We want to help people with their pains and their tragedies. Often we are confronted with not knowing what is wrong or with not knowing what we can do about it. It is this sense of helplessness that calls out our "answering service." Usually, when we are faced with a lack of awareness or knowledge we tend to find fault with ourselves. We feel inadequate. So the "answering service" is brought in to relieve our sense of helplessness.

The problem introduced by "answering services" is that when we indulge in them we are no longer in the moment with the other person. We need to find out who they are and where they are and, if possible, imbue them with some sense of hopefulness. When we feel helpless we transmit that sense of helplessness to the other person. Hopelessness is contagious. They catch it from us.

The remedy for these problems is that we find out from the client/patient where they hurt, what they want to achieve by coming to us, what they have done about it thus far, and what gains they get out of keeping things as they are. That keeps us in touch with the client/patient. Then we can, alongside that person, consider the alternatives and make decisions about present and future actions.

Answering Services are not necessarily bad. They provide information and give us time to decide on a course of action. It is important, however, that we not proceed arrogantly with our learned course of action: that we take the other person into our confidence by clearly stating what we do and do not understand and our hope of gaining an understanding by and by.

Assertiveness and Aggressivity

THERE is confusion between the two terms, Aggressivity and, Assertiveness. The former suggests a militant behavior with a disposition to dominate. It is characterized by demand. Aggressivity is a synonym for Angry Behavior. Assertiveness, on the other hand, suggests self-confidence in the expression of one's feelings, thoughts and behavior. It is not pushing one's self on others.. It is, by decision, allowing another person to hear what I am feeling, what I am thinking, what I am observing or what I am doing. Decision always plays a part in assertiveness.

All behavior that expresses one's self contains an element of fear. Aggressive behavior is fueled almost completely by fear-threat. It is OK to behave aggressively in games. So in baseball, we value the aggressive base runner who crashes into the base-man in an attempt to knock the ball out of his hands. Or in business games we consider the "self-confident," even arrogant, sales-person to be an asset. Such behavior, as in all aggressive game-behavior, is fueled by the fear of failing or the fear of losing.

Assertive behavior, on the other hand, is fueled by fear-hope. It is constructive in relationships and is characterized by a lack of defensiveness. It values feeling both in self and others, is concerned with understanding the situation clearly and, is most effectively expressed in the form of "I'd like(s)..." The Italian language differentiates between two forms of desire. "Voglio" (the present indicative form of "volere") means "I want" or "I wish" and is considered to be a harsh, aggressive statement of desire. "Vorrei" (the present conditional form) means "I'd like" and is considered to be a more courteous, less demanding, i.e., an assertive statement. It is used when relationship is of prime importance, as when giving an order to a waiter in a restaurant or requesting an appointment with someone. Always it is partially fueled by hope.

The essence of aggressive behavior is demand. Demand is an inward stance signaling a determined unwillingness to lose or to lose face or to fail. It is OK to demand when time is of the essence or when faced with a matter of life and death but only if you can enforce the demand. Otherwise demand almost always leads to disappointment.

Aggressivity represents a determination to be important in the eyes of other people. It is the type of behavior we find in the first attempt of a person who feels subordinated or second-class to establish himself in a community. When assertiveness training began it was customary to teach people to assert their rights in a demanding way or to diminish in their own minds the stature of an authority. So trainees were told that if your supervisor seems too powerful, visualize him in his underwear and thus reinforce your own potency. That type of training didn't work because first, if it empowered you, it did it by setting up an uneven playing field rather than equality and second, because it was almost always an unsuccessful technique. Some assertiveness training still fails to distinguish between assertiveness and aggressivity.

Assertiveness does not seek to elevate oneself by putting the other person down. It begins with an awareness that it is OK to be me and it is OK to decide to let other people know what I feel, what I think, what I am doing, what I am observing and what I'd like. Note well the part that decision plays in this process. It is not OK to blurt out anything that comes to my mind. Before I speak assertively it is necessary to process what I am going to say, considering whether it is fear or fear/hope that fuels the statement and the consequences that may result.

OUTBURSTS OF ANGER

SOME people come to me because they are troubled by little outbursts of anger in their relationships: sarcasm, sniping remarks, small manifestations of hostile behavior, or perhaps, a recognition that at times they would just like to make another person feel bad. They want to know what causes these outbursts and what they can do to control them.

Sarcasm is made up of a dual message. At the literal or social level the message is one of recognition or understanding and may be even complementary. At the psychological level it conveys doubt or carries insult and it always discounts some other person. Sniping remarks are recognized at once as criticisms. Using sarcasm or snide remarks to get a point across can become an habitual behavior.

• Sometimes hurts are allowed to build up for hours, days or years of frustration and the proverbial straw that breaks the camel's back releases the pent-up flow of anger. So a father who has commuted two hours from work to home, gotten a ticket for turning the wrong way on a one-way street and has just realized that he left some important papers at the office, greets his teen-age daughter, who is watching television, with, "I'm sure you have finished your homework!"

• Sometimes a given word or action breaks into the unconscious mind with a repeat of a threat felt in childhood. It may be a suggestion that reminds one of constantly being told what to do by one's parents.

• Sometimes a smoldering resentment that has been unfocused suddenly finds a safe outlet. Some people resent the weather, stew about the snow or ice, or the cold or the heat. Such stewing generates steam that eventually blows into sarcastic or disparaging remarks.

• Sometimes there is a distrust, generated in the past, of certain types of people or of the attributes observed in another person, e.g. distrust of certain kinds of women or men, or of smugness, or of a show of superiority. So, if I feel that I have been consistently rejected by blondes, I may make catty remarks about blondes in general.

• Sometimes there is a momentary disappointment or embarrassment, or a feeling of being discounted or violated or excluded.

• Sometimes outbursts of anger arise when a word or behavior threatens with a fear of failing or of losing face.

• Sometimes there is felt a need to "teach" another person and a sensing of his/her resistance.

Often hostile remarks are disparaging reflections on an absent party and contain a humorous edge. A five-year-old who is showing his mother how he can do a forward somersault and land on his feet, and who has said, "This is what my father used to do!" elicits a sarcastic remark from his divorced mother, "Sure, that's when he was in the circus!"

These are the same generators that provoke large outbursts of anger. Usually they are easier to uncover when the outbreak is a huge eruption.

The way to prevent such outbursts is first, to recognize the rush of adrenaline that prepares one for it. The level of energy rises, there is a slight flushing of the skin and a feeling of needing to defend. It happens so quickly that usually we miss these signs and so the next best thing is to stop in mid-sentence in the outburst and decide to act differently. It may take 10 seconds or so to get in touch with the threat and accept it as threat, then to decide what to say or do.

Speaking from experience, I know that there are times when I do not catch the signals until after the outburst. When that happens, the only thing I can do to salvage the situation is to back up and start over after admitting that I spoke hastily and that I regret it. That is also good pre-programming for the next time I feel the urge to lash out in sarcasm or a disparaging remark.

As for the desire to simply make someone else feel bad, that arises out of the same fear-threats that prompt the outbursts. It is, however, more repressed and often is the result of a long-term suppressed feeling of being violated. So, a woman who has been violated since childhood in the sense of being discounted, treated like she is nothing more than a sex-object, working in a comparable position as a man and being paid less, feeling like "Somebody almost walked off with all my stuff," may feel good about inviting some other person to feel bad. Because she has lived with the feeling of being violated so long, she no longer feels a rush of adrenaline at the crisis moment; she is constantly prepared to cut another person down. A remedy for that is to become aware of feeling violated and recognize it as the fuel which feeds the behavior. In the recognition and the acceptance of the feeling she establishes a modicum of control and the change in behavior will modify her feeling of need to hurt someone else.

About Agoraphobia

AG o ra pho' bi a is almost exactly what it describes: phobia, meaning fear or excessive fear and, agora, which refers to the ancient Greek marketplace. The agoraphobic has a crippling fear of almost every space that is not his every-day-existence space. Thus many women confine themselves to the limits of their home and perhaps a nearby small shopping area. It is probable that most agoraphobics are women, perhaps because of their childhood training, which tends to make them more fearful of strangers and exposure.

Agoraphobia is a complex phobia as opposed to a simple phobia in that the person who has the fear usually has other morbid fears, e.g. the fear of flying, the fear of exposure, the fear of crossing bridges, the fear of high places. In Ted's life agoraphobia included the fear of stores and malls, the fear of flying, the fear of crossing bridges, the fear of exposure, the fear of going out of control and the fear of dying.

Simple phobias, on the other hand, are usually confined to one or two excessive fears: the fear of spiders, the fear of insects, the fear of dogs, the fear of the sight of blood, or the fear of high places and are not as disabling, and they are often more transient and more amenable to therapy. Usually they are not revealed to companions or therapists unless, because the feared situation is unavoidable, they become disabling. One can avoid snakes or dogs if one is afraid of them but when the thing feared is a freeway and the one who is afraid must use the freeway to get to work, the fact that it cannot be avoided may cause the fearful one to communicate her fear or even seek help in overcoming it.

All of these individual phobias carry Latin names which I try to avoid, with the exception of agoraphobia, because the Latin names seem to clutter the landscape and make the fears seem like some formidable disease when in fact most of them tend to be transient and to cause little interference in a person's life unless it is a fear that is unavoidable. For example, many children have a phobia of animals, dogs or cats or birds, that goes away with the passing of time.

Usually multiple phobias are not verbalized in the first few therapy sessions. For example when agoraphobia is accompanied by other phobias, one is not usually in touch with the other fears because of the overwhelming fear of leaving one's home until, at the suggestion of the therapist, one dares do it.

There appears to be some commonality in the personality types of agoraphobics and obsessive-compulsive persons. Each has an avoidance pattern. The phobic avoids the feared object or situation, e.g., in the agoraphobic the fear of open spaces or market places. In the obsessive-compulsive person it is the avoidance of the fear of contamination, the fear of making an error (e.g., failing to lock the door or turn off the electric stove) or the fear of not maintaining a ritualistic behavior (e.g., the compulsion meticulously to arrange items on a desk in a certain way.)

Both the agoraphobic person and the obsessive-compulsive person are afraid of losing control (or of being controlled) and both seem to fear that a decision to change behavior may result in harm to themselves or to some other person.

Each of these two types is characterized by non-decisive behavior and are passive-resistive. Both are given to denial of their own power to change. They feel helpless.

In short both of these types are defiant personality types. In dealing with them it is important not to contest or even suggest that they change their behavior. I have found, in dealing with defiant people that giving them permission to feel whatever they feel, permission to think when they are feeling and permission to decide to make changes when they are thinking and feeling can enable them to control their behavior and get on with their living.

As to what precipitates a phobia there is very little understanding. Freud thought that it was caused by the child witnessing the primal scene between his parents and, while that does seem to enter in to some phobic manifestations it is by no means present in all and, at any rate does not account for the onset of symptoms. The onset of agoraphobia appears to occur usually between the ages of 20 and 35 and often is accompanied by a severe panic attack.

A thirty year old wife of a state patrolman reported that her first awareness of her agoraphobia occurred about three months after seeing a wrecked, burning automobile, with the driver trapped inside and policemen trying to free him. Her first awareness of fear was manifested in a sudden onset of terror on opening a closet door,, and from that moment on she was terrified of closed doors. She rapidly closed herself in her home, afraid to go anywhere. She related the fear of closet doors to having been punished by being locked in a closet as a child. She thought her fear of going out of the house was related to the fear of riding in an automobile that was subject to being wrecked and burning.

A twenty-five year old single woman reported that while walking on a down-town street she suddenly became terrified. She had a full-blown panic attack lasting some fifteen minutes with difficult breathing and a pain in her chest. She was not aware of anything that could cause such terror, but afterward, she was afraid to walk anywhere outside of her home.

A medical doctor reported that his fears began on the fourth floor of the university while dissecting cadavers. He was sitting close to a large window and became obsessed with the idea of jumping out of it. This was not accompanied by a panic attack but was consistent for the entire semester while he was engaged in dissection. He endured this obsession until it developed into agoraphobia and interfered with his practicing medicine.

The therapeutic approach to phobias is always to introduce the phobic person gradually to the feared behavior. In the fear of flying, therapy may begin with a discussion of air travel and airplanes and the feelings that occur when faced with the opportunity to fly. It may continue with driving to the airport and watching the take-off and landing of various planes. Behavior is never forced on the individual. He/she decides when to act. Over a period of time, the suggestion is made that the only way to deal with the fear is to accept it and to consider a trial flight. Along with these procedures there is always a discussion of the underlying fear of being not in control, of giving one's safety and life into the care of other people.

In agoraphobia, therapy involves the same kind of gradual introduction into entering the "market place." It may begin with visualizations and techniques of desensitization, e.g., "Close your eyes and imagine that you have decided to leave the house and go to the corner of the next block. Let me know by raising one finger when you first sense the anxiety." Repetitions of this technique with gradual extensions of territory lead to an actual experience of going out of the door. Once the front door is passed there comes an awareness that it is possible to deal with what has been an overpowering fear.

Overcoming phobic reactions does not mean ridding oneself completely of the fear. It means building confidence that you can deal with it and that it can become your friend, warning you of harmful extremes, e.g. going for a drive in subzero weather without a full tank of fuel and proper clothing in case you have a breakdown.

There have been situations where visualization techniques have worked in very brief therapy. Usually, however, the process is gradual and may take several weeks or months for the individual to gain the confidence needed to relax and enjoy the previously feared experience.

ON BEING DIFFERENT

MOST of us feel that we are different from other people. Sometimes young people feel that they are in this world for a special purpose: to right wrongs, do away with inequality and poverty, teach people a better way to live. A feeling that "I am special" can be a compelling force for change.

Each of us is, of course, different from every other. The combination of genes in our physical makeup stirred together with all of the minutiae of relationships in our individual environments plus the traumatic experiences we undergo and the parental messages we receive form a person as different from other persons as a snowflake is different from other snowflakes.

Sometimes this feeling of difference is a major cause of depression. Feelings are the major elements in a depressing belief that "I am different." When a child is consistently told by precept that he should not feel, ("Don't cry!", "That doesn't hurt!", "You know you don't hate your mother!"), or by example, (father and mother never express emotion), he grows up believing that, because he feels, he is different from other people. That belief, in the Child ego state, takes the form of "I ain't like other people."

"I ain't like other people," means, "There is something wrong with me." Other people don't think about sex as much as I do, other people don't lose their temper, other people don't feel bored in church or school, other people aren't prejudiced, other people read faster, understand more of what they read, remember things that I forget, succeed where I fail...etc.

A simple switch in one's perception of oneself can make a huge difference in attitude. A client who had grown up in a strict and religious family came to me at age 32, depressed and suicidal. She was a missionary assigned to a South American country and she was sent home because of her depression. She expressed her problem as one of being different from other people in the missionary enclave. "I long to kick up my heels a bit, to enjoy life and to teach other people to enjoy it. I'm not like the rest of the missionaries. They are industrious, hard working and sober in thought and spirit. I don't fit in to that world. I don't fit in with my family. I don't fit in to proper society." She spoke of her mind wandering during prayer service to things she would rather be doing than praying. She spoke of being bored while listening to sermons. And she felt she was the only one who was distracted when she "should have been" devoted.

One day she came in with a different attitude. She walked erect with her head held high and she was bursting with enthusiasm. "I found the answer to my depression," she said. "It's not that I'm not like other people. *It's that there's nobody else in this world exactly like me!*"

That switch in thinking made a major change in her life. From, I ain't like other people! to, there's nobody else exactly like me! set up a different framework in which to see herself. Now, she feels that it is OK to be an individual, different from all the rest. That it is OK to feel anything she feels, and OK to decide what to do about what she feels.

The negative side of being different is that I have no right to be different. I have no right to feel and think and decide and enjoy and relax. It is life governed by "oughts" and "shoulds."

The positive side of being different is that we can revel in the joy of being a distinctive person with all of the rights and responsibilities and capacities that go with it. It's OK to be me!

A Loan?

One of the curious things about money is how it can sometimes be disruptive to a friendship. I know a brother and sister who did not speak to each other for several years because the brother decided to pay his sister's part of a family expense. I have seen lovers split up because the man loaned the woman a little money. I myself have lost a friendship because I loaned my friend a minuscule amount of money.

What psychological factors come into play to alienate friends and siblings and lovers when a small amount of money is at stake? First of all there is the natural inclination of the recipient to feel like one who is being rescued by someone who has means that he, the recipient, does not have. That casts him in the victim's slot of the Karpman Rescuer, Persecutor, Victim triangle.

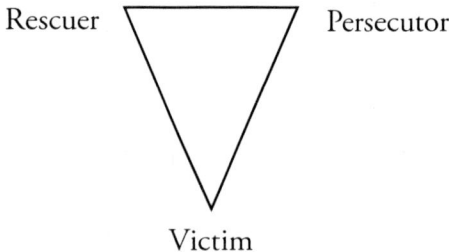

Rescuer   Persecutor

Victim

Most of us do not like to admit that we're victims even though we feel like we are victims. It makes us uncomfortable to realize that the one who has rescued us can now shift roles to criticize us. That fear may be escalated into hostility causing a rift in the relationship between the provider and the recipient. A second dynamic that enters the equation is guilt. The party receiving the donation or loan feels some sense of inadequacy in re-paying the provider. Even if it is a donation, we feel we are indebted. No one of us enjoys feeling indebted. We may even think of reasons why we have not or should not repay. The provider has so much more adequate means than we have or he owes me for a favor I did for him. The longer the time interval the deeper the guilt, particularly if the provision is in the form of a loan. Soon the mere sight or thought of the provider invites me to feel guilty and guilt, being so oppressive, naturally escalates into resentment. I find myself resenting the provider!

These two factors, a feeling of inadequacy and a feeling of guilt, are the basic dynamics of the hostile behavior which is displayed either in withdrawal or spite.

To insure oneself against such hostile behavior I suggest that if the amount of money is substantial a written contract stating the exact terms of repayment be drawn and signed. If the amount is minimal consider making it an outright grant and impressing that fact upon the recipient. If the other person is reluctant to take the gift do not insist. That smacks of rescuing, and rescuing is only advisable when the matter at hand is concerned with life and death or when time is of the essence.

Finally, if hostility does result from the transaction, speak to the recipient about the matter; tell him what you'd like or, if it is a demand and if it can be enforced, what you demand. That at least will clear the air and allow the relationship to be reconstructed if it is possible to reconstruct it.

If, on the other hand, you are the recipient of the favor and feel some sense of inadequacy and/or guilt, speak to the donor about your feelings. In the acceptance of feelings and the decision to speak about them openly, there is foundation for a healing of the relationship.

Addictions and Compulsions

RECENTLY a client spoke to me of being "addicted" to a love relationship. She explained that she had been to a weekend workshop where all kinds of addictions had been discussed: addiction to work, addiction to driving fast, addiction to love, addiction to sex. She wanted to know how to get relief from such addictions, particularly her "addiction" to loving a certain type of man.

This points up a widespread contemporary misuse of the term "addiction" for what is more accurately termed "compulsion." The difference is long-standing and by definition.

Addictions are, by definition, characterized by physiological dependencies. There is some evidence that they may be linked with certain genes that predispose a person to a particular dependency. So statistical analyses indicate that twenty to thirty percent of the American population have a predisposition to alcohol abuse.

Compulsions, on the other hand, are characterized by emotional and ideological dependencies. Addictions always take the form of compulsive behavior but compulsions are not always addictive and when they are, they may be said to be psychologically addictive.

Drug counselors differentiate between addiction and habituation. Habituation refers to the development of an increased tolerance for a given substance with or without a psychological dependency.

One may be habituated to a substance such as caffeine or nicotine or sugar and/or physiologically addicted to it. One may be habituated to sex or love or driving fast or work but those habituations take the form of compulsions driven by an ideological or emotional need for power or security or preservation of selfness with an accompanying sense of inadequacy.

The concept of "obsession" tends to cloud the dividing line between addictions and compulsions because obsession usually is present in both. An obsession is a persistent thought that disturbs one's equanimity and moves one toward some form of relief. So, when an alcoholic abuser thinks of sailing, he/she is pre-occupied with buying beer for the cruise until he/she buys it. So also, the person in love is pre-occupied with the need to see and touch the love-object. Obsessions normally result in adjustive behavior whether they are the result of addictions or compulsion.

Since both addictions and compulsions usually result in objectionable behavior, it is important to recognize that while the obsessive need-feelings cannot be blown away by will-power, the undesirable behavior is always subject to the individual's control. It is important for the addictive or compulsive individual to understand that he/she can stop the unwanted behavior, that it is not impossible to stop drinking or smoking or over-eating and that it is not impossible to curb one's behavior-habits of loving, sex or work.

The differentiation to be kept in mind is that addictions are derived from physiological needs and compulsions are derived from emotional/ideological needs. And the reason for the psychotherapist to differentiate the two is that "addiction" is a much more frightening term and tends to make the compulsive lover, driver, worker feel more helpless in overcoming his/her compulsion.

How to Start a Conversation Anywhere

SOME people are so self-conscious or so preoccupied with the fear of failing that they have difficulty starting or carrying on a conversation. "I never know what to say," is their complaint. It can be a reason to avoid parties or dating or even getting together with friends. In starting a conversation it is always important to remind yourself that the other person may have similar self-doubts as to his/her conversational ability.

There are some things you can do to start and/or extend a conversation.

In order to do it you need concentrate on: 1) the other person, 2) feelings and 3) situations. Let's say you approach another person at a party.

1. Concentrate on the other person. Be complimentary. "I like your tie," "Those are beautiful earrings." Ask questions by making observations. Start with an impersonal question such as: "I guess you are a friend of the host?" or "You live in this city?" Then you can proceed to ask more personal questions such as "I'd like to know about your (work, family, interests.)"

2. Concentrate on feelings. What am I feeling and what is the other person feeling? In your approach to the other person ask yourself, Does he/she appear to be feeling interested, anxious, angry or bored? Know that one of those four feelings is probably uppermost in the other person's consciousness. One choice of starting a conversation is to say, "You seem (happy, sad, resentful, lost in thought." You need not be absolutely accurate in your perception to invite a response. It is enough to be close enough to touch on the other person's feeling. In order to do that you may need to sharpen your awareness of feelings by observing other people. Does the person in front of you in the grocery check-out line, seem to be frustrated, or anxious, or patient? How about the persons seated next to you in church or theater: what do you perceive they are feeling? Once you are adept at perceiving what others are feeling, you have at hand a comfortable option to open conversation.

And don't forget your own feelings. Are you feeling anxious. Let the other person know it. "I usually feel anxious at parties like this." Or if you are enjoying yourself? "I enjoy meeting people and talking with them." Try to match your feelings with what you perceive in the other person. "I'm a bit tired this evening and a little bored."

Since I'd likes are feelings, it's OK to mix in a few of those also. "I'd like to talk with you," "I'd like to have a cup of coffee (another martini, a place to sit down.)" And ask the other person what he/she would like. "What would you like to do on your next vacation?" "Would you like another drink?"

3. Describe a situation. "I saw you standing here alone." "It's been a (beautiful, rainy, cold, hot) day." "There's hardly anyone here that I know." "There are lots of people in this small room."

Such openers tend to elicit response. The "I like your..." invites the other person to explain where or how he/she got the admired object. Impersonal questions expressed as observations generally call for a response that contains information that can move the conversation along.

Stating what you perceive the other person is feeling usually leads to a clarification by the other person of what he/she is really feeling or why the feeling is present. Stating your own feeling or saying what you would like may call for agreement or disagreement. Either way you have produced an item for conversation.

Describing a situation reveals an interesting observation that the other person may or may not have noticed and offers a topic that can be amplified by both the other person and you. Speaking of today's weather can be amplified to include this month's weather or the weather around the world. Mentioning the immediate situation in an objective way might be amplified into "The last party I went to was in a huge room." which could be extended to questions about where that party was, etc.

These suggestions work just as well when you meet someone for the first or the fifty-first time. Keeping the other person in mind, thinking in terms of feelings, and describing situations provide not only an avenue of intercourse. They also bring out interesting information. And who knows, they may even lead to a lasting relationship.

CYNICISM OR SKEPTICISM?

A synonym of "skepticism" is "uncertainty." It means a belief that a particular item of knowledge is subject to doubt. From where I sit, that seems to be a rather helpful attitude toward understanding life particularly where religion, political statements or any other form of "fact" is presented as fact. It may be because I was born and raised in Missouri, the "Show Me State," that I am aware that there are generally more than two sides to any question. Or it may be because of a kind of defiant temperament that leads me to doubt any statement made as "fact." When I was a child it seemed to me that there were two kinds of knowledge. There was a stack of things that everyone knew were true. It was a very short stack. Then there was a stack of things that human beings were not so sure were true. That was a very tall stack. And what has amazed me through the years is that someone is forever removing an item from the first stack and placing it on the second.

I had to face such uncertainty in my religious faith. From my childhood I thought it was equally unfounded to say "I know there is no God" as to say "I know that God exists." It is much firmer ground to say, "I do not believe in God," or "I do believe in God." Belief does not establish fact!

I had to face such uncertainty in my pursuit of psychology. Was Sigmund Freud espousing fact or theory when he re-discovered Oedipus?

I have also noticed that in a declaration of a belief, loudness and emphasis betray some doubt on the part of the declarer.

So, I place myself among the agnostics both in religion and psychology, certainly in any governmental decree or in any institutionalized project. Defining an agnostic as one who is not certain that a truism is a fact, I find myself in that category. I am a skeptic.

I am not a cynic. Cynicism, no matter how thinly it may be defined, implies a lack of faith in people. The day before I left home to go to college, my father and I drove out by the local lake, parked and talked. I remember one thing he said. "Son, never lose your faith in people!" That stayed with me. My father, who knew at least one severe betrayal by one of his closest friends, gave me that rule to live by. It has kept me aware of the potential in every human being to grow and make the changes that are needed.

When Franklin Delano Roosevelt referred to "...those cynical men who say that democracy cannot be honest and efficient..." he was incorrect either in the adjective, "cynical," or the object. To correct it, substitute "skeptical" for "cynical" as the adjective, or "who believe that men in a democracy" for "who say that democracy" as the object. "Skeptical" would imply a lack of certainty about democracy as an institution and thereby open democracy to questions. I believe there is wisdom in questioning any institution. "Cynical" implies a lack of belief in the honesty and efficiency of the human beings who make up a democracy.

The true cynic can never be a happy person. Happiness requires some minimal trust in other human beings. Skeptics, on the other hand, can be obsessed with their doubts and still enjoy living.

Most of us are skeptical at times and cynical at times. It is important to know the difference so that while maintaining a healthy skepticism, we can guard against become habitually cynical.

POMPOSITY

Do you often find yourself caught in the middle between two or more people in making arrangements or attempting to settle a dispute? Placing yourself in the middle usually occurs with 1) making arrangements for a future event, 2) listening to a complaint about a third party or 3) a request to mediate in a dispute. It always indicates passive behavior on your part and the part of others involved. How did you get there? What is there about you that invites others to make you an intermediary when there is no necessity for it? And how do other people invite you into being in the middle?

Perhaps you are pompous. That is you have a heavy Need to assert your own importance. Pompous people find it difficult to delegate responsibilities without a showy surveillance of what is being done. They need to let people know that they are part of the action and want to be consulted about everything that is done, and that their suggestions are always important. It is not so much that they don't trust others to complete a task. Rather it is because they want to be in on every decision.

The roots of that kind of Need to interfere with the mechanics of every operation, be it a family argument or arrangements for next month's office picnic, are deeply embedded in a feeling of being responsible for everybody and everything. They probably stem from childhood. Often they are initiated by an early felt responsibility for a younger sibling, sometimes they arise from feeling responsible for one or both parents. Whatever the roots, the behavior which places one always in the middle, brings with it an impatience and an anxiety about the use of time and energy. Middlers generally feel that they are pushed for time and often feel worn out by their many responsibilities. It is true that the time and energy could often be used to greater advantage in taking responsibility for oneself, one's personal enjoyments and in taking time to relax.

Sometimes such interference in situations that are not your true responsibility is invited by passive partners. So a wife tells me that her husband refuses to answer the telephone and that she "has to take messages about arranging the softball schedule in which he is involved." She often takes two or three messages in an evening and "finds" herself anxiously calling other team members to find out what is an acceptable time for her husband's team to play. Given her own passivity in making herself available for such yeoman-service, her husband's passivity is a strong inducement to it.

She found the solution. She became assertive. Whenever she received a call she would respond, "You'll have to speak to Michael about that. Yes, he is here but he refuses to talk to you at this time. I'll tell him you called." So Michael had either to assume his rightful responsibility or give up his leadership position in softball, and she was relieved of the anxiety about arrangements.

Complaints to you about another person tend to place you in the middle. The assertive response to, "Have you noticed how Jim spends half his time on personal phone calls?" is "I'd like you to speak to Jim about that." That takes you out of the middle and avoids the prevalent office game of Let's You and Him Fight. (Incidentally, know that anyone who criticizes someone else to you will also criticize you to someone else!)

Often the interference by the pompous one is resented by one or more of the principals involved. Even though they invited it they don't like being controlled by a middle party. A teacher who was meeting with a special group of students for thirty minutes each week, was told by another teacher that he should increase the time to one hour. His reply was, "If I do that I shall expect you here next week at the end of my half-hour to take over the group for the final half-hour!"

A pompous need to mediate is sometimes caricatured in comedy. Two people refuse to speak to each other. Although both are present they call on a third party to relay messages between them. I have witnessed it in families as when an older sister telephoned her younger sister to tell their widowed mother that, at her age, she should not be dating. Again the assertive response is, "I'd like you to speak your own feelings to mother."

Pomposity goes hand-in-hand with the need to take care of other people. If you often find yourself mediating between two parties or constantly caught in the middle of arranging future events, it may be time to examine your motives and correct your false beliefs that only you can solve other people's problems or make correct arrangements. Knowing that your importance is based on who you are and how you relate rather than on being involved in everything that goes on is your ticket out of the middle.

THE PROBLEM OF "PLEASE!"

TEACHING children to say, "please," which is intended as a polite way of asking for something, can exacerbate a low self-esteem problem in a large number of people as they grow from childhood through adolescence to grown-up living and sharing. Used incorrectly it tends to place the person requesting something in a subordinate position as though his/her welfare in some way depends on the goodwill of another individual. It smacks of pleading for a favor.

Millions of people believe they are not deserving of the goodwill of others. That starts in childhood when "deserving" is equated with "earning." Since the child does not "earn" any income he/she is dependent on the adults in the household, particularly the parents. "Deserving," of course, is not a synonym of "earning." Children deserve to have the basic necessities of life furnished them even though they didn't earn them, along with being loved and nurtured.

Sometimes, when I am speaking to a group of clergy-people, I ask them to define the "grace" of God. Almost never do they define it accurately. Almost always they render it as the "undeserved" favor of God. Not even the older catechisms say that. Instead they state that "grace" is the "unearned" favor of God. After all, we did not earn the beautiful things that surround us in nature, nor did we earn the love and care that we received from our parents, nor even life and health. We do deserve those things, however, even if we do not receive them.

We deserve the care of our parents not because of what we do but because of who we are. We are their children. In the same way, we deserve the unearned favor of God, or of whatever brought about the beauty of the earth, because we are children of God, or children of whatever caused the splendor of nature.

So, we deserve the favors of our peers, even though we may not have done anything to earn them. If I am at table and I would like the butter passed to me I should not feel that I am subordinated to the potential passers. When I say, "Please pass me the butter," it is as though I am pleading with them to favor me by passing it. In my mind's eye I see myself on bended knee, begging for them to appease my wish. In my mind's eye, I see myself as unworthy of their effort.

How much better for me to feel that we are equals! With that feeling I may say, "I'd like the butter," or even "I'd like the butter, please, " because "please" added at the end of a request is not a subordinating expression but an added courtesy. Try it on your own tongue and notice the difference. Imagine you are speaking to someone who has just entered the house and you would like him to close the door. "Please, close the door," sounds dependent, "I'd like you to close the door, please," makes for a level playing field. To preface a request with "I'd like..." adds to my feeling of deserving because it is an assertive statement. To add "please" to the end of the assertive statement adds a touch of graciousness which I can afford to provide because I am an equal.

So, "please," used unwisely, seems to diminish the speaker in his/her own eyes while "please," used correctly and not for the sake of "politeness" adds a pleasant and polished note to the request.

LOVE AND AFFECTION

"I love" is most certainly an ambiguous phrase. It has so many different shades of meaning. It can mean anything from "I like" to "I am enraptured"; from "I have goodwill" to "I am deeply involved in the happiness and contentment of..."; from "I am sexually stimulated" to "I cherish our moments together."

In fact the Greeks had four words for "love:" agape, phileo, eros and storge. Most people are pretty well versed in the meaning of Agape, "goodwill," Phileo, "brotherly (or familial) love" and Eros, "sexual excitement," and not at all aware of Storge, which translates as affection.

Usually we are attracted into a permanent commitment to another by eros. Something about the other person triggers our hormonal flow and we become sexually excited by our thoughts about the "loved" object. It may lead to marriage or a long-term commitment. The advertising media exploits eros by posing beautiful people in commercials and promising successful romantic interludes if we use the advertised product. The other three kinds of love are not calculated to make us want to buy anything and so advertising neglects them.

When religion speaks of love it usually is in terms of Agape: "goodwill." The Golden Rule may be interpreted as "Have the same goodwill toward others as you would like others to have toward you." At its most perfect manifestation it means a kind of thoughtful consideration for others that is not diluted by ill-will shown to me. In a lesser form it may appear with any of the other three Greek concepts of love.

Phileo is the kind of caring experienced among blood relatives, mothers and fathers and children and cousins and other family members. "Blood is thicker than water" means that family members have a kind of regard for each other that is not found among strangers. "Philadelphia" is the "City of Brotherly Love."

And so we come to Storge. Affection is normally felt in the beginnings of sexual excitement, sometimes in familial relationships and even occasionally in feelings of goodwill. Affection is the kind of love that endures. If a marriage is to endure happily, it is imperative that as the sexual excitement ebbs, affection develops and grows. Affection means, essentially, "I like to be with..." I have a dog, a beautiful Golden Retriever. Her name is "Lacey." As I write this in my study, Lacey is lying close to me. If I move to my office, soon I will hear her coming down the stairs to be with me. When I go outside, she follows me through the door. She has affection. She wants to be with me.

Agape gets to be routine and is often felt as an obligation. Phileo grows thin at times under the stresses of family disagreements. Eros grows into boredom. (Consider how much less interesting it is the 75th time you see your lover unclothed.)

Storge, on the other hand grows with use. "Out of sight, out of mind," applies to eros. "Absence (or presence) makes the heart grow fonder," applies to storge. Affection is a major component of the term "love." It is the part that holds families together and allows any of our relationships to flower.

GENTLE CONFRONTATION

CONFRONTATION need not be harsh or brutal. It can be done in a way that reveals caring. Gentle confrontation is confrontational but not aggressive. Many people fear to confront another person's life problems because they equate confrontation with rudeness or roughness. That is often an accurate description. When group work began in the early nineteen-fifties it was almost always true. Confrontations were judgmental, accusatory, and often brutal. The idea seemed to be that if one threw enough shit in a person's face, and that person was able to withstand the onslaught and come up smiling, it was a sign of insight and growth. The problem was that so often the criticism was not accurate or even realistic, and even if it was, it left a sore place and a scar on the individual's psyche. That technique was followed rather closely in the EST seminars, where people were put down until they had had enough and defied the agent. It was training in how to become rebellious and aggressive. It did not teach people to be realistic in their own confrontations or in their responses to confrontation. It did not teach assertiveness!

Confrontations are based on what we perceive to be destructive patterns in another person's thoughts, beliefs or behaviors. In facing that person with our perceptions of such destructiveness it is important that we be tentative rather than dogmatic. "It seems to me that you tend to withdraw when faced with conflict," is gentler than "Why do you always with-draw when faced with conflict?" The latter is accusing the other person's unconscious and he/she will tend to react to that ac-cusation defensively either by agreeing or denying rather than discussing what has been perceived.

Gentle confrontation may be describing a situation as a camera would have registered it, without criticism or judgment. "You have received four suggestions from the group tonight and you have dismissed each of them." is gentler than "You have rejected everything that has been suggested to you to-night!" The first is what a camera would have seen. The second is judgmental because of the term "everything." The implica-tion is that the individual is a negative person who does not accept any suggestions thoughtfully.

In gentle confrontation it is important to face the indi-vidual only with what is perceived as fact. "You have had three DWIs (driving while intoxicated), is gentler than "You are a dangerous driver."

The one who is doing the confronting also needs to handle confrontations of him/herself non-defensively. Confronted with, "I don't think you know what it's like to be six-months pregnant and having to work nine hours a day!" the non-defensive, thera-peutic response might be, "You are right. I'm sure it is not easy for you and you are responsible for how you deal with that."

It is never gentle to ask short, jabbing questions, one af-ter the other. Such as "What did you do?" "What were you thinking of?" "Why did you do that?" Faced with questions like that anyone would feel backed into a corner and be more concerned with what the questioner might do with the answers than considering how he/she could have acted more appropri-ately. In fact, it is better to make tentative observations than to ask questions, particularly when you know the answer.

Gentleness requires strength. That is, you must have con-fidence in yourself if you are to be gentle. Bravado, in which one, masking weakness, comes on like a bulldozer, is never gentle. What is required is an acceptance of yourself and an awareness that you might be wrong coupled with a willingness to take the risk because you believe that you are perceiving the situation correctly.

Gentle confrontation is an art. It requires a non-judgmental stance that does not contest and does not dilute reality. It requires assertiveness rather than aggressivity and it requires that the confronter does care about the person being confronted. It is not shoveling shit at a person in the hope that when it is wiped off, the person will be better for having survived the onslaught. It is perceiving facts and providing them tentatively to the individual who needs to hear them.

FATHERS AND MOTHERS

IT may seem politically incorrect to point out that there is a vast difference between fathering and mothering. There is a vast difference in the traditional patterns, there is a substantive difference in the equipment available for use, there is a qualitative difference in the kind of care offered and there is a quantitative difference due, in part, to present exigencies. Patterns of parenting have been dictated in large part by the fact that women come equipped to bear children and breast-feed them. It was natural for the woman to play the larger part in nurturing the child. It was natural for the man, free of the burden of bearing and nurturing, to move outside the family circle and become the major provider of logistics. It now seems natural, whether because of brain-sidedness, or long usage, for mothers to be more concerned with relating to the child while fathers are more concerned with solving immediate problems on a rational basis. Mother nurtures. Father confirms.

Father became used to working outside the home more and more remote from the family and mother became used to protecting the family in the home. So it became normal for father to be away from the children while mother held her children close.

All of these factors have been altered to some degree in this day but the patterns still exist. Although he is closer to the family than before, it is still mother who does most of the housework, cares for the children's health needs, does most of the chauffeuring to Little League and martial arts and dance classes and altogether spends more time with the children than does father. This leads to a kind of remoteness that characterizes most of our thoughts and feelings about our male parent. Most of us have a somewhat subconscious yearning to be closer to our fathers. At the same time we already feel close (sometimes, too close) to our mothers.

When working with a group of people, if I speak at some length about "mother" I see pleasant expressions of remembrances on the faces of most of the group. If I speak about "father" I witness an expression of wistful yearning on those same faces, sometimes a tear appears.

In a survey done in Los Angeles about fifteen years ago, high school seniors were asked about their fathers' occupations. A large majority of them did not know what their fathers did for a living. Most of them thought of father as the provider who left home in the morning before they did and returned home after them in the evening.

This kind of remoteness characterizes the feelings children have about their fathers. In thinking of my own father, a Protestant minister, who spent most of his time working with people outside the home, two of my fondest memories are of going fishing and hunting with him. When I think about it, I can remember only three occasions of that. Once we went fishing together. Once a group of us including an uncle and a cousin went on a one-week fishing trip, and one time my father and I went squirrel hunting. Yet those memories are among my most precious thoughts of my father and with them comes a felt yearning for more of the same.

So we feel a closeness to our mothers and a yearning for, and a remoteness from, our fathers. As one of my clients expressed it, "I hold my mother, and I yearn for my father to hold me."

MANIPULATION

BECAUSE I believe that the essence of effective relationships is authenticity, I struggled for years with the awareness that I manipulate people. Every transaction with others is a manipulation. When I say something to you, it is with the expectation of some sort of response. In other words, the purpose of my communication is to elicit a response and by framing my words in a certain way I predict your rejoinder. If I am predicting your response then I am being manipulative! All conversation thus consists of predicting what the other person will say when I say what I say. And thus all conversation is manipulative!

So it is not the fact that we constantly manipulate other people that is odious. It is a particular characteristic of the manipulation that makes it acceptable or unacceptable in relationships. That quality is whether or not the manipulation is a discount. When it does not take into account the significance of one or either of the concerned parties' feelings, thoughts or behavior it is a discount and is probably destructive to the relationship.

So it is not the manipulation but the discounting that destroys the authenticity of the exchange. This makes it possible for me to accept the fact that I can manipulate others without the deception that is often manipulation's hand-in-hand companion.

Passivity

I differ somewhat with the usual definitions of the word, "passive." It is usually defined in some terms of "inactive," yet be aware that one of the most destructive forms of passivity is known as "passive-aggressive" behavior which, by definition, may be active.

I define "passive" as non-decisive, non-goal-solution oriented and aggressive. The passive person is apathetic; tends to let other people and situations control his life. He may also act-out his fear-threat and angry feelings, e.g., being late for appointments or spilling his drink on the hostess or her chair or carpet. He does not think of how to solve basic problems but rather acts in ways that avoid immediate confrontation or stress. Passivity is always aggressive in the meaning of angry or hostile behavior. The anger may be turned inward on himself producing depression or guilt or it may be turned outward on other people in a manifestation of sarcasm, resentment or rage.

The opposite of "passive" is "decisive." The decisive person may be either aggressive or assertive but she is not apathetic. She is self-actuated, proactive rather than reactive and in charge of her own life. She uses her Adult ego state as the decision maker and she can decide to be child-like or parental when the situation is perceived as calling for it. Her aggressivity is usually goal oriented and her assertiveness is always goal oriented.

While there is a preponderance of passive behavior on the part of both sexes, my perception is that it is a heavier masculine than feminine trait. In men it is usually a part of their defiant anger patterns. In women it is more likely to be a part of their frustration anger patterns. Masculine passivity tends to be directed outward in competitiveness. Feminine passivity tends to be directed inward so that a woman may be oriented to take care of situations at the expense of her own dignity or feelings of self-worth.

Relationships, whether familial, communal, national or international, are not furthered by passivity. Passivity does not make any relationship better. It may gloss over the problem as when a woman subordinates herself to her husband for fifty years of unhappy but quiescent existence.

It is decisive behavior that changes relationships for the better. In my own practice I have seen marriages markedly improved by either the husband or the wife deciding that he or she does not intend to put up with the old patterns, thus awakening a desire for change in the other partner.

Part of assertive behavior is knowing what you'd like and deciding to let another person know about it. Until you know what you'd like it is impossible to be decisive about achieving it.

TRUST IS A BEHAVIOR

Trust is essential to any close relationship. For that reason, when a trust has been violated, it often seems impossible to reestablish a coherent association. A husband who discovers that his wife has been unfaithful may feel it is impossible to trust her. A parent who discovers that his 10 year-old son has been stealing change from her may feel that it is impossible to trust him. Yet it is widely understood that when we trust a person it tends to develop trustworthiness in that person and not trusting another encourages him/her to develop into an unreliable individual. So a dilemma is present. What to do? The answer is, if you want the relationship to flourish, you must trust the "unreliable" person.

This is easier to do when you understand the difference in the meaning of two words: "confidence" and "trust." "Confidence" has to do with feeling while "trust" has to do with behavior. I am traveling a rural road in an automobile that the manual says weighs 3500 pounds. I come to a wooden bridge with a sign that says, "This bridge will support 3500 pounds." It looks rickety to me and the sign appears to be of a ripe vintage. My confidence in the bridge and its endorsement may be lacking. Whether I cross the bridge depends not on my confidence but on my trust. If I trust the sign I will attempt to cross the bridge in spite of my lack of confidence.

So reestablishing a relationship can be done even though

you lack confidence in the other person if you decide to act in trust. After all, your confidence in the original formation of the relationship was due to a lack of contrary experience rather than on a factual basis. So the re-establishment cannot be based on factual knowledge. You can decide to trust. That does not mean that you will not have attacks of doubt. It means that under the siege of doubting you will reestablish your decision to trust. It means that you will not resort to spying to check on a spouse's activity. It means that you will not place temptations in the other person's line of vision. It means that you will not count the quarters in your purse so that you can entrap the 10 year-old. It means that, in spite of your doubts you will assume the trustworthiness of the other person until you have substantiating evidence of his/her betrayal. It may seem naïve not to seek to verify your trust. The problem is that if you look for contrary evidence you are almost sure to find it. That search never ends. A lack of evidence does not satisfy the untrusting person. He/she continue the search until something damning is found. And in the very search the foundation for the re-establishment of trust is destroyed.

The old Russian proverb that translates, "Trust and Verify" is applicable to certain situations such as in business dealings: contractual obligations and services that require payment, but in human relationships verification is first of all, difficult to achieve and secondly, destructive.

Know the difference between "confidence" and "trust." If the relationship is important to you don't demand an impossible confidence but rather, act on trust.

LOSS OF MEMORY OR PREOCCUPATION

IT seems to be true that as people grow older they tend to be more forgetful. They misplace papers and can't remember where they placed them. They lose their keys. They don't remember names very well. They even forget appointments.

Several years ago I began to be forgetful of names. And then, one day, I took a vacation from my work and went to a hidden resort area in Southern California. It was an interesting place and I was relaxed. During the day I met seven other visitors, spoke with them briefly and enjoyed making their acquaintance. To my surprise, when I returned home in the evening I remembered each one of their names. What was the difference? I think it was that during that day my mind was relaxed rather than occupied with data. It never even occurred to me that I should remember the names of the people I met.

Thinking about it, I remembered hearing Dr. Karl Menninger speak about playing the game of Concentration with his five-year-old grandchild. In that game cards are laid out face down and the idea is to turn up cards that match in the least number of tries. Dr. Menninger said that he had played the game numerous times with children and that he could never win. Why should that be so? I think it is because the child's mind is less cluttered with internal dialogue than the contesting adult.

Each of us, as we grow older, has many feelings and thoughts crowding each other for our mental attention. Many of these are in the form of things we should/should not have done and things we should/should not be doing. In working with psychotherapists I often ask them what messages they have in their heads when doing therapy. They all confess that they have concentration-disturbing messages: "I should already have heard that," "If I knew more about this type of problem I should be better able to deal with it," "I hope the client doesn't recognize that I am about to fall asleep." Some have even told of messages that indicated they were in the wrong profession: "Maybe you should have been a truck-driver instead of studying psychology."

So, as we grow older, our minds become more cluttered with things to do and once the fear of loss of memory begins it acts as a self-fulfilling prophecy. I am so afraid that I won't remember that I cannot think of what it is I want to remember!

This is the problem of "pre-occupation." There are certain remedial actions:

1. Lead an active mental life. Learn a language, study advanced mathematics, work cross-word puzzles. The advantage of such activities is that one is constantly reassured by an awareness of how sharp the mind actually is.

2. Practice relaxation techniques such as the Relaxation Response or self-hypnosis or guided imagery. Here the advantage is that for a short period of time the internal dialogue is reduced or discouraged and the mind is allowed to clear its "desk top" and cope with current events.

3. Engage in aerobic exercises at least three times a week for thirty minutes each time. This allows more of the blood, that usually stagnates in the abdomen, to flow freely to the brain cells that are responsible for memory.

4. Give yourself positive suggestions about your memory. "I have an excellent memory" encourages an excellent memory whereas "My memory is failing" lowers a cloud over the mental processes.

There are a few people in whom there is deterioration of the mind affecting memory, e.g. those who are afflicted with Alzheimer's disease and probably many more whose memory is disturbed by prescribed medications. My suggestion to them is that they consult with a physician. But for most of us, it is not a failure of memory but a mind filled with preoccupation, largely in the form of internal dialogue, that causes us a major discomfort.

And for these, take heart! You are not "losing your mind!" This very reassurance is enough to help most of us regain enough of our memory to practice the mental exercises that will bring us even more reassurance that we can remember what needs to be remembered.

WHEN THERAPY FAILS

THERAPY consists of three major phases. The person seeking help comes because of feelings that are not comfortable. He may be depressed or agitated, feeling that he is oppressed or that he is out of control, feeling misunderstood or that he is responsible for others in an exaggerated sense. He comes because he feels he has a problem. This is the feeling stage of psychotherapy and it consists of exploring, clarifying and understanding what the uncomfortable feelings are about.

This exploration takes the participants into the second stage of psychotherapy: the thinking stage. Here we thoughtfully explore the causative factors behind the troubled feelings: childhood experiences, family patterns and relationships, current difficulties, mental and temperamental factors. In other words we have passed through the initial feeling stage to an intellectual stage and we intellectually consider anything we think is applicable to the client's problem. Some people don't like to intellectualize. But how else can we consider prior and present patterns that have formed the issues which the client wants to resolve? Intellectualization is proper so long as it is not used as a substitute for feelings.

It is in the third stage of psychotherapy that most of the failures lie. It is comparatively easy to discover where the client is hurting and the patterns of his life that have caused the hurt. It is far more difficult for him to take the action necessary to resolve the problem. This is the doing stage. When, by decision, the client changes his behavior, the feelings are changed. And here is where one needs to look when therapy is failing. I may know the intellectual reasons for the uncomfortable feelings I carry about but unless I change my behavior I will still be subject to the discomfort. Of course, understanding why I feel the way I do and the knowledge that it is OK to feel what I feel may bring some comfort but to change the feeling requires that I make some sort of behavioral change.

These then are the three stages of psychotherapy:
- the feeling stage when affect is most important
- the thinking stage when intellect is paramount
- the doing stage when behavior changes.

Each of them is important. The third one is crucial to the success of most therapy.

Boxes We Live In

ALL of us live in boxes. Boxes have sides or limitations. They are usually built by parental or societal expectations.

The are both restrictive and protective. So a box keeps us from touching a hot stove. A box may also keep us from enjoying a week of vacation with a touch of luxury.

One Sunday afternoon in Norview, Virginia I decided to trim the shrubbery in my back yard. I was snipping away happily when I noticed a delegation of three people approaching my backyard fence. Since I had only recently moved into the neighborhood I anticipated that this might be a committee welcoming me to the community. Instead, what I heard was a reminder that "people in Norview do not trim their shrubbery on Sundays!" That was my introduction to one side of the box in which the residents of Norview lived. Since I had come from Denver, where Sundays were used very freely to work or play, I was not accustomed to the limitations of the Norview box. I had a choice to make: to go along with the local custom or to rebel. I decided to conform in the belief that a little bit of adjustment can produce a lot of harmony.

A few years later I was doing a workshop for the Naval Drug Rehabilitation Center in Jacksonville, Florida. Every Saturday there was a meeting of the Officer-in-Charge with all of the residents in which they were encouraged to express their complaints. At one such meeting a resident complained about having to get up at 6:00 o'clock every morning and having nothing to do until 8:00 o'clock when the day's activities began. He asked if it were permissible to lie down on their newly-made beds and sleep for an extra hour. The Officer-in-Charge thought for a moment and then said, "There will be no lying down on your bunks after you arise at 6:00 o'clock." I followed him into his office and asked, "What is the reason for your decision?" His response was immediate.

"I can't get them to eat breakfast!" he said. Then he smiled and said, "My mother used to say that everyone should begin his day with a good breakfast!"

Most of us know something about the "breakfast box." We are a little uncomfortable with our usual fare: coffee and rolls, or a quick cold cereal when we "know" we "should" eat a "good" breakfast.

If you are a Roman Catholic you have certain perimeters around sexual behavior that are different and although you may not stay within their bounds you feel a tinge of guilt when you disobey them. If you are a Southern Baptist you may have had similar limits placed on dancing and card-playing. Breaking out of such limits can cause a touch of uneasiness of the conscience or at least bring on an awareness that the boundaries were at one time established.

Belonging to any group brings with it certain provisions of behavior that are supposed to be followed. Some gangs insist on at least one felonious act for membership. All churches have certain rules that are understood by those who are devoted. Political parties are the source of another set of regulations that one is expected to respect.

One of the problems of living in boxes is that we do not always judge correctly the size of the box. For example, if the Roman Catholic box is this size:

some of the more scrupulous people might interpret it as this size,

thus restricting their behavior even more than the church intends.

So it is important to know how much room I have to maneuver within the box and to know that I have to have an uncontaminated awareness of what the limitations are.

And what if I want to get out of the box? There are two ways: one by impulse or compulsion which represents sociopathic or psychopathic behavior. The other by decision which usually represents growth. The sociopath and psychopath recognize no established boundaries in certain areas of their life. Their box may look like this:

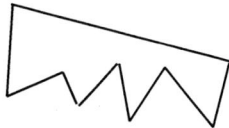

Their reactions may be impulsive or willful. They are always based on the easiest way out of the immediate dilemma. So they act on expediency rather than on fact or consequence and the sociopath, especially, is usually pretty adroit at sidestepping the results of his behavior.

Getting out of the box by decision is moving outside in a response of reason and after considering what the consequences may be. The consequences may be threatening, even fatal! Consider the fate of Martin Luther King or Mahatmas Gandhi.

Most of the boxes we live in are restrictive only to a minor degree. When the box becomes oppressive it is time to consider whether it is worthwhile to attempt to improve my lot and/or the lot of others by moving out of it.

WHY BEGIN AN ADDICTION?

WHAT motivates us the very first time we take a drink or light a cigarette? For the average person the first step in incurring a habit that may become an addiction is for one of only three reasons. It is either 1) a feeling of peer pressure, 2) a need for social lubrication or 3) adopting the style of a model. There are a few people who, out of curiosity about the effect, may be attracted into a first-time usage. Among these there may be artists who have heard that drugs or alcohol frees one from inhibitions and allows one to express his feelings in his art. These are not the average first-user persons who act out of the three reasons listed.

The first one takes the form of "Everybody I feel close to does it! To be socially acceptable to them I need to conform to their ways." So if everybody in my social group drinks or smokes I do not want to be different and risk alienation from them. There is powerful motivation to conform to the protocol of the group, particularly among teen-agers. So, today, the wearing of baggy clothing and the adoption of unusual hair styles are rages copied by a large group of adolescents. And so, when all of my friends are drinking alcohol or smoking, those behaviors become a part of the group design. In order to belong I adopt the manners of the group. That is peer pressure.

The second reason takes the form of "I am self-conscious and nervous when I try to socialize with people. Maybe a little alcohol will give me enough confidence so that I can relate more freely." And of course it is true! Alcohol tends to suppress the limiting dialogues that constrain our freedoms. After a drink or two I no longer worry about what I say and under the influence of one or two (or a dozen) beers what I have to say seems to make more sense and is much more humorous. To test this out, sit down at a bar and drink ginger-ale and listen to the conversations going on about you. You will be surprised at their inanity and their lack of wit. That's because you are sober. If you were sharing the same spirits that the speakers are, you might consider what they are saying as filled with meaning and humor.

In a similar manner, lighting and holding a cigarette, gives one a sense of doing something meaningful as one attempts to relate to other people. Part of the habit of smoking is due to the feeling that "It gives me something to do with my hands!" As long as I am busy I don't think so much about what I am saying or doing. And besides that, for some people, schooled in movie and television glamour, smoking is associated with being sexual and seductive.

What about these first two reasons for taking the first drink or lighting the first cigarette? Well, of course, they are faulty because they preclude assertiveness and self-improvement. If I can belong to a group without asserting my differences, I learn submissiveness on the one hand and defiance on the other. Both of these are reactions rather than responses to life situations. In order to make changes that improve life, it is necessary to be responsive and pro-active, rather than passively reactive.

The same is true when we consider lubricating our social relationships by dulling our awareness. To enhance our self esteem requires that we learn to relate to people without resorting to drugs or artifices.

In other words, neither of the two reasons for beginning

an addictive behavior has any legitimacy when compared to taking decisive action to correct our felt inadequacies. Far better that we take steps to change ourselves than rely on dulling drugs or preoccupying behavior to smooth out the rough places for us.

As for the third reason it speaks more to the model than the follower. Most of us have idols with whom we would like to be identified. For some of us it may be the Marlboro man, for others a Gloria Steinem or Martin Luther King or a father or mother or a sports figure. Models have a certain responsibility to personify healthful ways of living.

While each of us is responsible for our own behavior in all three reasons cited, in the third instance that responsibility is shared by the model. While I am not "my brother's keeper," I bear some responsibility when, through my behavior, I invite him into an addictive pattern that is destructive.

Why do we take our first drink or light our first cigarette? For most of us it is because of a sense of inadequacy in ourselves. Since everyone, early in life, feels this sense of ineptitude or inferiority most of us are tempted to deal with it by bowing to peer pressure, lubricating our social interactions and seeking identification with a model. Some of us. because of other forces at work within our psyches will move from those behavior patterns into addiction.

Mostly it is up to parents to invite their children into the knowledge that they are OK by praising even their modest successes rather than criticizing their mistakes and by being, themselves, role models that further healthful patterns of living and relating.

BE CAREFUL!

THE scene is this. You have spent the holidays with friends or relatives and now you are preparing to leave. The friends or relatives accompany you to the car and as you close the door and start the engine, they lean in through the open window and say, "Now John, be careful in driving home!"

"Be careful," heard so many times when we are children, carries a fearsome message. It says, in effect, "Something terrible is about to happen!" That message puts us on our guard, makes us watchful and a bit nervous.

Driving back home at the end of a labor day week-end I heard the following message on my car radio: "The death toll on the nation's highways now stands at 548. The National Safety Council predicts that there will be 590 people killed before the holiday period is over."

I glanced at my watch. It was 11:30 p.m. Thirty minutes to go and we still need 42 more! At that point I (and probably a few other drivers listening to the same broadcast) ran off the road! The message I heard in my head was, "Be careful!"

We need to "be careful" how we use the command, "Be careful." In fact it is my belief that the National Safety Council, in predicting the number of fatalities over a given holiday, poses a frightening scenario that may be self-fulfilling. That prediction scares us and makes us less confident and less competent in our driving.

This came to my attention when I was stationed in Japan with the U.S. Navy. One morning I was called to the Brig about 1:30 a.m. As I entered the front gate of the compound I was suddenly confronted by a ghastly scene. Two bodies covered with what appeared to be blood lay at the curb with an overturned car on the side of the street. I stopped, got out of the car and investigated only to find that it was a mock-up of an accident. The annual Far-East safety campaign was scheduled to begin that day!

Shocked by the scene I called the senior shore patrol officer for an explanation. I asked him to research the history of the safety campaigns and tell me what the results were. Later that day he called me and told me that to his surprise there was an increase in accidents during each of the thirty-day safety-campaign periods over the past five years. I called the Marine Officer who was in charge of the local safety campaign and explained to him what I had discovered. He replied that there was nothing he could do about it. A postscript. The local activity won the award that year and on the way to receive the recognition the Marine Officer collided with a train!

There used to be a program, sponsored by insurance companies through local police departments, of showing safety films to drivers who had been ticketed for speeding or reckless driving. These were not Driver Education films. They were films that showed horrible accident scenes, in effect showing the viewers fifteen ways of causing accidents. It is my understanding that Texas Insurance Companies seeking to determine actuarial statistics on automobile fatalities, once did a survey to determine the effect of showing safe-driving films to drivers. The control group consisted of people who had not viewed the films. The surprising result of the survey was the finding that those who had seen the film had a higher accident rate than those who had not!

The essence of this argument is that scare tactics do not change behavior for the better but for the worse. In the early days of governmental intervention in drug abuse, a trailer was rigged with all kinds of frightening furnishings including a coffin. It toured the country. Later, in the analysis of statistics it was discovered that almost immediately after a visit to a city, drug abuse increased in that city. Or consider the effect of trying to get cigarette smokers to stop by scaring them. Almost all Stop Smoking organizations reject scare tactics as an effective method.

It appears that it is more effective to encourage people to consider what they prefer instead. Instead of reckless driving, I would prefer personal safety. Instead of smoking I would prefer to live a long and healthy life.

Of course when it is a matter of life and death and time is of the essence it is OK to say, "Be careful!" On all other occasions it would be beneficial to say, "Go safely!" or to make some other positive suggestion.

Doing Your Best

"The least one can do is to do his best!" appears to me to be a trap that leads either to false grandiosity or to guilt.

What is my best? To do my best in one endeavor would mean giving that effort every bit of my waking time to the exclusion of all other interests. To feel like I owe a task my best results in feelings of guilt if I fall short. It would be more realistic to speak of doing a task well or fairly well and it is far more realistic to know that that is all I ever need to do. It is always grandiose to say, "I did my best."

"I did my best." is often used by perfectionists as an excuse for failure. It is as though, "I did my best, but..." Former President Jimmy Carter used it that way. After a failure in diplomacy he would say, "I did my best." Of course, Jimmy Carter was a perfectionist. He was compulsive about doing everything "right." And that was probably why he got mired down in details. Some matters call for delegation. Some call for a minor effort. Some call for a major effort. The perfectionist has difficulty distinguishing which is which. To the perfectionist, "Any job worth doing is worth doing well!" It is not so much that he/she wants things done "perfectly." It is more correct to say that he/she wants things done "right," and by right is meant "the way I want it done."

For people who are driven to do everything "right," guilt is a frequent visitor. They often find themselves going over in their mind what they "should" have said or done and being haunted by their omissions. This is crippling to their future endeavors. Instead of noting their failures and deciding to make changes in their behavior, they obsess about their past mistakes. Guilt does not further changes. Judgements made on oneself or others seldom results in betterment!

It is well to know that everyone fails sometimes and that it is OK to fail. That is, it is OK not to measure up to one's own standards. And it is certainly OK for other people not to measure up to your or my standards. In other words it is a wise person who knows that neither you nor I can ever do our best!

INTERDEPENDENCY

In these days when so much is said about dependent and co-dependent behavior it is worthwhile to examine the phenomenon of dependency-interdependency.

Some people speak of symbiosis as though it is always a pathological relationship. That is true when one of the symbiotic parties does not accept responsibility for his/her behavior or when he/she takes on responsibility that is not rightfully his/hers. That sets up an unhealthy dependency relationship, an unhealthy symbiosis.

There is a cycle of dependency-independency which we learn as children. It can be diagrammed thus, going around the circle to the left from the bottom:

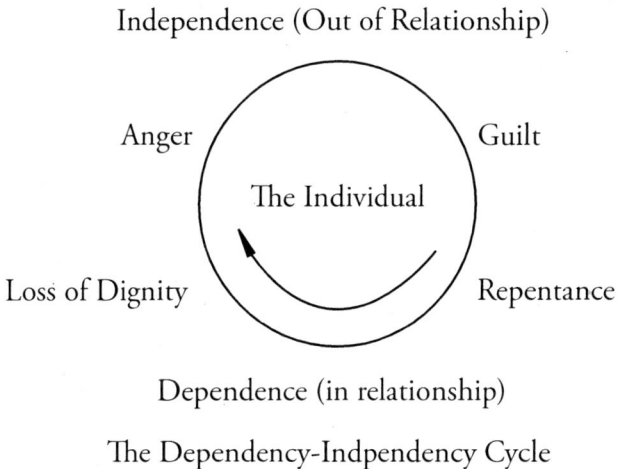

Independence (Out of Relationship)

Anger   Guilt

The Individual

Loss of Dignity   Repentance

Dependence (in relationship)

The Dependency-Indpendency Cycle

Quite naturally, when we are small, we learn that we must be dependent on larger people (the bottom of the cycle). That brings a comforting feeling that we are in relationship with higher powers. It goes well enough until we begin to sense a loss of personal dignity. At that point we feel inadequate and the sense of inadequacy is escalated into anger, first in the form of defiance, and then in the form of resentment. With the anger comes a sense of potency and we begin to feel independent (the top of the cycle). We may feel strong and good about that for awhile until we sense that our independence places us out of relationship. At that point we begin to feel guilty. Eventually we repent of our resentments and our feelings of power and, seeking forgiveness, find ourselves again in a state of dependency. This might be thought of as the religious cycle because it reflects what happens in a religious person who relies on God for guidance and strength.

Most of us struggle with the back-and-forthness of needing dependent relationships and the need to feel independent. It feels demeaning to be dependent; it feels great to be able to depend on someone else!

Co-dependency is the habitual, unhealthy relationship that exists when one does not allow himself/herself to own the responsibility for his/her behavior. It always takes at least two people to play the co-dependent game: one the rescuer/persecutor and the other the victim.

Interdependency is a kind of healthy symbiosis known as "mutualism," a mutually beneficial association between two people, in which each relies on the other for certain services with mutual regard for each other's capacities and limitations. In our infancy it is the "quid pro quo" between mother and child. The child gives to the mother a glow of pride and hope. The mother nurtures the child. In adult life it may be a sharing of household chores or fiscal responsibilities by mutual consent. In a sense, then, interdependency is the mutual trust formed between two persons, each of which comes equipped with special talents and willingness to meet their part of the trust.

JUST SAY NO!

As a psychotherapist there are two questions sometimes asked by clients to which my immediate answer is "No!"

The first of these is, "Should my mother come and live with us?" The answer to that question is always "No." Then it is up to the questioner to justify his/her mother's presence in the household. There are some circumstances that moderate the answer to "perhaps" or even encouragement to do it. Some exigencies necessitate that mother be welcomed into her son's or daughter's home. When such exists, I encourage the participants to make the best of the situation and enjoy her presence. My initial answer, however, is "no!"

The second question to which my immediate answer is "No!" is more controversial. It has to do with marital infidelity in which one of the spouses has had an extra-marital sexual encounter. Often that spouse has a heavy sense of guilt or shame and they feel that they will feel some relief if they "get the matter off their chest." Recognizing the enormity of the impact on the other, they seek information on what the effect might be and whether they should deny the affair or admit it. Should I tell my partner what I have done?

My first question in response to that question is to explore with the individual what his/her reason would be. If there is a need to confess in order to relieve feelings of guilt I suggest that a confession will not erase the behavior and that very likely it would complicate the problem. Next to our name our sexuality is the most sacred part of our psychological make-up. Almost everyone has some doubts about his/her own sexual adequacy. To have, what is seen as, a sexual betrayal constitutes a grave offense against one's personal image, which is already in question. In other words it makes one doubt one's own adequacy as a sexual partner. Rather than admit such doubt we tend to escalate it immediately into resentment of the offending party. The hurt can be so enormous that it presents a chasm of doubt and anger that can seldom be successfully traversed.

There is another reason to deny the extra-partner affair. It may awaken a vengeful reaction in the other partner to follow a similar course of action: to have an affair of his/her own. In years of working with groups I have often asked for an indication from anyone who has never been tempted to lust after someone other than a spouse. I have yet to receive such an indication! It is my belief that the propensity for a sexual encounter outside the primary relationship is present in every human being. And that is particularly true after being in the relationship for several years. If the desire for revenge, coupled with the inclination to "see for oneself what it is like," is activated, then obviously the problems within the relationship are intensified. Sometimes the reason to confess is a need to "get even" with the partner who may have had a similar offense earlier on. Such a reaction, clearly, would deepen the problem.

But how can I justify encouraging a complete falsehood? To answer that I admit that I justify the encouragement of not being totally honest in other facets of a close relationship. Sometimes it is brutal and damaging to a relationship of affection to be honest. If your husband gets a disfiguring haircut just before an important business conference, do you tell him that it looks terrible? Or do you tell him that it doesn't look so bad, so that he enters the business negotiations with a bit more confidence in his appearance?

And this falsehood regarding marital/partner infidelity speaks to encouraging confidence rather than mistrust. When I know that my partner has been unfaithful it is harder to trust him/her in the future than if I only wonder about his/her behavior.

Further I justify the encouragement of denying any sexual infidelity by my experience with those who have confessed. It has almost always led to a complete disintegration of the bonding which here-to-fore existed. Mary, having been counseled to deny a marital infidelity which had occurred eight years in the past, in order to relieve her guilt, told her husband what she had done. He, being a very religious, professional man, after much weeping, told her that he understood and forgave her. But now a wound had been opened and he began to infect it with his own doubts and suspicions. He felt betrayed, and he wondered about his own sexual sufficiency and, above all, his lack of sexual experience with other women. He came to the counselor with his doubts and his fears and the question, "How can I trust her not to do it again?" He thought of his own marital decency and began to question its worthwhileness. Six months later he went to bed with the wife of his best friend, came home and told Mary what he had done. From there the feelings of betrayal and guilt and inadequacy and anger escalated until the divorce three years later. In the meantime the distraught husband and the distraught wife went from bed to bed without resolving their own feelings or solving their own problems.

I never dictate that the answer be "no" to either of the two questions. After all, the goal of psychotherapy is that individuals take charge of their own lives by making their own decisions. I point out the problems that saying "yes" bring into play and hope that, in their wisdom and common sense the individuals involved will decide, in a constructive way, their course of action.

THE NEED TO QUANTIFY

IN reading professional journals I am often struck by what I see as a need to quantify the unquantifiable. Some things are subjective and cannot be reduced to linear equations. Among them are attitudes, feelings, temperaments, and decisions. Part of the reason for this monograph is the conclusion I reach after attempting to read the journal articles which, in their mechanistic approach, seem both unusable and un-useful in the practice of psychotherapy. Some of them are so convoluted that they leave me shaking my head and wondering how their intricacies could be applied to actual practice.

I remember an address given by Ken Boulding, well known Professor of Economics at the University of Colorado, in which he spoke of economic predictions. He said that he had researched the major economic predictions made for the past 100 years and had found not one of them to be correct! So even such "predictable" matters as economics and demography are not totally quantifiable.

The need to quantify is a result of the struggle to be scientific in our observations of human behavior. Most of what we write about people, their emotion, their thinking, their behavior, is concerned not with what can be objectively measured but what can only be subjectively understood. The attempt to linearize such subjective contents can only lead to approximations of reality.

As scientists are discovering the random quality of data, so sociologists and psychologists and even medical researchers need to be aware that they too, cannot place infallible trust in exponential extrapolations of building blocks.

Just as physical scientists profited by Newtonian "laws" until they began disassembling the atom, so those of us who deal with people can profit to a point in the "laws" of human nature. In life structures, however, the variables are so astronomical in number that, even as we progress, we need to be aware of how tentative are the conclusions we reach. As someone has said, "Take three observations of a comet and three of a cat, and it is safer to predict the date of the comet's return than to predict which way the cat will jump!"

So this is a call for practical, easy to read, essays that portray what the practitioner perceives happens in psychotherapy and reports his perceptions in a style that is both admittedly subjective and is easy to understand. After all, what Einstein is reported to have said about the universe seems applicable to all of life. "When I stand at the edge of the universe and look out it appears to be more like a great idea than a great machine."

FINANCING SECRECY

In dealing with family-members or friends it would seem to be a good rule-of-thumb not to finance secrecy. This first came to my attention when a father kept reporting that he had paid another term's tuition for his daughter in a Junior College. I asked him how her grades were and he told me that he was unable to find out since she was 18 years old and the college refused to disclose her grades to anyone other than the woman herself. It eventually turned out that she was not in school at all, that she enrolled each term and did not attend any classes. It was not the only time that the father had financed secrecy.

After all, a person who is supporting another has a right and, sometimes, a responsibility to know what he is supporting. This does not mean that he has a right to know all the details. If he trusts the recipient enough he may not be concerned even about the general use of the funds provided, except when the inquiries he decides to make are met with consistent secrecy. Joe provided his daughter with a monthly contribution toward her apartment expenses. He was also called upon to make substantial payments on her credit cards. In return for this help he received no information on the amount of her paycheck nor what she had purchased with her credit cards. When he inquired how much she was paid or what major credit-card expense was for he received non-committal responses. Further, he had reason to suspect that she was a habitual drug user.

The question one needs to ask is this: is there an overt unwillingness to discuss the usage made of the funds provided? If there is (and barring such special situations as birthday and holiday gifts that may be intended as a surprise) then it would appear wise to clear the air by saying, "I am unwilling to finance secrecy."

ACTING CRAZY

WHEN my son was 10 years old he came home one day from school with the announcement, "Dad, my teacher is crazy!" He explained what he meant. She had assigned four pages of identical problems for homework in arithmetic. "Why have four pages when one page would be enough?" was his question. I explained to him that it did seem "crazy" to assign so many problems and that since the world out there is sometimes crazy, it is important to know that we can go along with it by deciding to act "crazy" ourselves. "That means that I have to do all four pages," he said. I agreed that that is what it meant.

How often in the crazy world of communication a decision to act crazy furthers our goal! I have spoken some abusive word to a friend and the friend responds, "You didn't mean that!" To which I respond in a crazy way, "No, of course not." To respond sanely in a negative way, to that negative inquiry I should have replied, "Yes," meaning "Yes, I didn't mean it." But it goes much deeper than that.

Let's say that I work for an organization with assigned tasks and duties. And let's say that while the work day is from eight to five, I finish my work by three o'clock. The sane thing to do would be to leave my work-table and go home. But that isn't the way the organization sees it. So I have to stay, idle though I may be, until five.

Or let's say that at three o'clock in the morning I come

to an intersection just as the light turns red. There is no traffic. The sane thing to do would be to ignore the light. But I sit there for two minutes and forty-five seconds while a meaningless evolution of switches controls a non-existent flow of traffic. That kind of craziness is dictated by the knowledge that the traffic cop sitting partly concealed behind the corner filling station does not excuse rational decisions.

So, over and over, in daily situations we have to decide to act crazy and go along with the system or bear the consequences.

THE MEANING OF SIGHS

A sigh is an audible communication. It says something to the one who sighs and to anyone listening in. The message always has to do with feelings.

One message that a sigh transmits is, "It's over," or more correctly, "I feel like it's over." It is heard at the end of a trying experience, like driving home in a beating rainstorm or even at the end of tiring day.

Mary has just learned that her husband of 28 years is having an affair with a young woman employed in the office. As her mind races over the past, the initial romance, the children, the happy times and the sad times, she sighs deeply communicating the feeling, "It's all over." Notice that the feeling may not reflect actuality. Her marriage may not be over. What the two of them decide to do about their lives and their relationship will determine that. But she feels that it is over. In response to the sigh I say, "So, Mary, you feel like a chapter is closing in your life." Whether or not her marriage is over, a chapter is closing in her life and it is well that she understands the correctness of her feeling.

Another feeling message, heard more frequently, that a sigh transmits, is, "If only..." It is heard when one considers situations or behaviors of the past or present and wishes that something was or could be different.

Jerry is speaking of being heavily into credit-card debt

and thinking of the things he bought that he could have done without. Somewhere in the course of his speaking he sighs. "If only..."

The psychotherapist registers any sighs that she hears and, if she decides not to interrupt the discourse, files them in her memory for later use. She knows that they have meaning and will bring them up at a proper time by saying, "I notice that when you were talking about your family a while ago you sighed deeply. What did it mean?" At times I may interrupt the client when I hear a heavy sigh. "When you were speaking of your son just now, you gave a deep sigh. I think it meant, if only... If only what?"

As with other non-verbal transmissions such as a smile or a frown, it is important for the listener to record and acknowledge sighs. The recognition gives the patient permission to accept the feeling that he/she has.

So, hear the sighs, record them and confirm them. It may lead to the opening of a new awareness It will do no harm and, in fact it is healing, to allow a person to know that it is OK to feel whatever they are feeling.

LISTENING

Dr. Karl Menninger has said that in spoken communication there is usually a subject and a predicate, and static. Static consists of all of the unnecessary words, the dilutions, the self-limiters, the grandiosities and the negatives that are thrown in because of habit and/or fear, plus the body language, which is usually more revealing than the words. He spoke of the importance of the "static" in hearing what a person is saying. How do we listen for the static?

Listening is an art that involves all of the senses. Because we have been trained since childhood not to listen while another person is speaking, but rather to engage in the preparation of a defensive response in case it is needed, we have lost the child-like quality of listening with all of our sense organs: eyes, ears, touch, taste and smell. Children, until they are told that it is impolite, listen with all five of the senses plus one other: their own feelings.

• Ears. Some of us hear principally with our ears. That is, we remember what we hear better than what we see or touch. It is always important to train one's ears to hear what is being said: the subject, the predicate and the static. Among other things that are important to hear are self-debasing words, grandiose expressions, diluting words, negative words and encouraging words. It is also important to hear what is not being said: the deletions and distortions that almost always accompany a conversation.

• Eyes. Others hear principally with their eyes. They remember what they see better than what they hear or touch. And of course it is important to train your eyes to see what is pictured. A young mother, who had been complaining about her husband's lack of attentiveness, came in for her session and this time she brought her reluctant husband and her fifteen-month old son with her. She was feeding the baby as she talked when suddenly the nipple came off the bottle and the milk spilled on my office floor. She immediately got down on her hands and knees and with a diaper and a towel set about cleaning up the mess. Her husband sat quietly, aloof from the action taking place. "This is what you wanted me to see?" I asked. She replied, "He never helps me with anything."

Other things to observe with the eyes is body language: the body twisted in the chair, indicating mixed feelings; the arms folded across the chest, indicating resistance; the legs squeezed together tightly with the arms across the lower abdomen, indicating a protective stance; a sudden pallor or flushing of the area around the mouth; a finger placed against the lips. Body language, observed by sight, is fascinating and meaningful.

• Touching. While most people are unaware of its importance, one touch can take the place of a thousand words. A clammy handshake tells me that the person is fearful in some way. A half-body presentation in an embrace, speaks of fear of closeness. If I touch your arm and find you are trembling I know that there is some kind of emotion involved. This is one reason I make it a practice, after inquiring if it is OK, to hug my counselees after each session. Another reason, of course, is because I like to hug!

• Taste. I don't know that I have ever tasted one of my clients but I can see how it might be valuable. The sweetness or saltiness of a skin surface might be useful in some way. At least, I don't rule it out.

• Smell. Don't neglect this one. In at least one rare case it opened up an elusive problem for therapy and getting well. Helen came to me with a major complaint about her dissatisfaction with her work, her boyfriend and her life in general. In the third session I decided to speak to her about her excessive use of a heavy perfume. She admitted that she liked to "smell good." "I also use a lot of pancake make-up," she said. "And, if I'm not mistaken, you also use a different hair-coloring agent each month," I responded.

"How come you feel the need to cover up with perfume and make-up and hair color."

"Well, I might as well tell you," she said. And she told me of having made two pornographic movies and of how disgusted she was with herself for having made them. She went on to speak of her feeling that she carried a stigma from those films: a persistent body odor, some facial scarring (she thought), and, because she had been a blonde in the two porno films, she "couldn't stand" her natural hair color. Without going into the therapeutic process I will tell you that that woman gained enough self-confidence to go back to college, then get a law degree and eventually teach business law in a university. And I think all of that result had something to do with my sense of smell!

• One's own feelings. Because everyone has the same feelings, differing not in kind, but only in degree, it is possible to pick up what another person is feeling by the way he invites you to feel. During a study of schizophrenic patients at the National Institute of Mental Health in the late 1950s there was a practice of de-briefing therapists after each session with a patient. The reason was because the therapist often identified with the patient, and came away from the session feeling schizophrenic. When one has accepted his own feelings and dealt with them sufficiently then one becomes empathic to the same feelings in another person. If he has not dealt with his own feelings he may deny them or he may be sympathetic rather than empathic.

When, in talking with another person, you sense yourself feeling lonely, or blue, or cynical, it may well be because you are identifying with that other person and picking up from him/her what he/she is feeling. To recognize that makes you a better listener.

Use all six of your senses in listening: your eyes, your ears, your sense of touch, your sense of taste (perhaps), your sense of smell and your own feelings. This is listening with the whole person.

TRANSACTIONAL ANALYSIS THEORY

THE HEART OF TRANSACTIONAL ANALYSIS THEORY

THIS paper begins with an observation and a question. The observation is that Transactional Analysis, as conceived and formulated by Eric Berne, was not so much a method or technique as a belief. The question which must arise in the musings of every person who knew Eric well, is **why did he die so young?**

I believe that the reason Eric died earlier than any of us expected is that he failed to plumb the depth of his most important belief: the OKness of being human. The affirmation of OKness is the heart of Transactional Analysis theory. Eric, himself, described it that way: all Transactional Analysis theory, he said, can be summed in the statement, "It is OK with me for me to be me and it is OK with me for you to be you."

Tom and Amy Harris publicized that concept in *I'm OK-You're OK*, (1967) That book, even more than *Games People Play*, (1967) focused public attention on Transactional Analysis and, more than any other writing to that time, opened doors to hope for thousands of people who felt hopeless and helpless. It did not offer very much practical information on how to affirm OKness and, in fact, reflected a kind of philosophical-theological vagueness about its meaning. In 1973, in a paper presented at the Summer Conference of I.T.A.A.. in San Francisco, I amplified the I'm OK - You're OK principle with what

I then called the "Perspicacity Formula" now referred to more frequently as the "Autonomy Formula."

I - Rt + Rsd + C to make decisions + TCOL

In the formula:

I = (every) Individual
Rt = Right,
Rsd = Respondability/Responsibility
(and)
C = Capacity
(to make)
= Decisions
(and)
TCOL = Take charge of his/her own life.

I have heard that formula quoted many times since then, sometimes incorrectly, i.e., leaving out the **Decision** symbol. In a complete form it may be stated in two other ways:

• Every Individual has the **right to make decisions** and take charge of his/her own life.

Every Individual has the **respondability and responsibility to make decisions** and take charge of his/her own life.

Every Individual has the **capacity to make decisions** and take charge of his/her own life and.

• Every individual has a **Child** ego state, a **Parent** ego state and an **Adult** ego state.

Eric, who consistently cautioned himself and others against being duped by metaphor (e.g. "I know this place like the palm of my hand."), in this matter, so central to his life and theory, allowed a metaphor to distort his thinking. Instead of pursuing the value of **humanness**, he pursued the metaphor of "princeness." *In Principles of Group Treat-Treatment* (1966) he wrote, "Every human being is born a prince or a princess; early experiences convince some that they are frogs and the rest of the pathological development follows from this."

Eric was carried away with the metaphor of prince and princess. He saw it as an ideal. As a child he fantasized holding court, gathering other children around him, much as in his adult years, his followers gathered around him in a kind of reverence and awe for his incredible insights into behavior and his brilliant intuitive powers. In a metaphorical sense, he **was** a prince. He was loved as a prince, set apart as a prince and as a prince, he had difficulty accepting strokes for **being**. Once, long before the book was written, I invited him to a party and he spoke openly of feeling awk-ward at parties in his honor. "I never know what to do," he said, "after I say, 'Hello.'"

Of course there is a problem in being a "prince." That is simply because it requires a mask, a posture of seeming rather than being. Human beings are not, in fact, princes and princesses. I am not a prince. You are not a prince. Queen Elizabeth is not a princess. It takes at least as much energy to wear a prince-mask as it does to wear a frog mask. Eric, who emphasized authenticity, undoubt-edly knew that, and yet he did not plumb its depth.

More than anyone else I have ever known, with perhaps one exception, Eric Berne believed in people. His statement, made repeatedly, that 100% of the population has an Adult ego state is an expression of his faith in the perspicacity of the individual. Yet he somehow felt it was not enough for **him** to be human. In Kahler's and Caper's terms, 1974) he was **driven**. He had to fulfill his scripting as a prince.

There have been attempts to identify Eric Berne's script. Claude Steiner, (1974) described accurately Eric's fear of strokes. Eric defined intimacy in negative terms and felt that it was ex-tremely fragile.

Perhaps it was not an accident that Eric never explored

one of the most famous and, certainly in the late 50's and early 60's, one of the most obvious script tales: *Camelot*. To read that story of King Arthur's court, of Guinivere and Lancelot, is to be struck by its parallels in the life of Eric Berne. Strangely enough, most people seem to yearn for a Camelot existence and miss seeing that it is not easy, happy, nor long-lived to wear the mask of a prince or princess.

Yet Eric affirmed it's OK to be me, and again, more than any other theorist of this generation, he championed the enabling of men, women, boys and girls to attain autonomy. He did that by believing that they could solve their own problems, heal themselves, get well, when provided with an authentic atmosphere.

This belief in the human person was at the base of a comment he made at every summer conference: "I wish you people would understand the difference in permission and injunction." He saw people needing permission to be. He cautioned against mistaking injunctions for permissions.

When I survey the present world of Transactional Analysis I am convinced that his fear was correct. Much of what is called therapeutic procedure appears to be overriding injunctions from the therapist's Critical Parent, rather than permissions from the therapist's Nurturing Parent.

The problem with injunctions is an obvious one. All injunctions carry a discount, sometimes subtle, of the object person's Right, Respondability or Capacity to make decisions and take charge of his/her own life. And all injunctions carry a message, "Don't Think!" Even the common hexagonal STOP sign carries a more complete message: "Don't Think! Stop!" And when we approach that sign at an intersection, automatically and without thinking we step on the brake. The sign seen occasionally on the office wall, "Think!" in its subtle completeness, says, "Don't Think!

The giving of injunctions is an attempt to structure the therapeutic process and the therapeutic process is essentially non-structured. Every attempt to structure it stems from the structurer's feeling of inadequacy. This does not mean that I am opposed to all structure. For example, I consider contracts essential to the therapeutic process. But I want the contract to be framed in an attitude of autonomy. The autonomous form of a contract is the infinitive form: to be, to do, to think, etc. It is the simple future and affirms the goal of the process, that the individual decide to make the change established in the contract rather than resolve to make the change at the therapist's suggestion..

I see the goal of all psychotherapy to be two-fold:

- That the individual comes to a compassionate understanding of his/her parents, of other people and of him/her self and,
- That the individual comes to take charge of his/her own life.

Eric's concept of *permission* is subject to much counterfeiting: injunction giving in disguise. Permission is enabling a person to be aware of the OKness of feeling, thinking, deciding, enjoying, relaxing, touching, being, risking, winning, relating, working, playing, changing, living, dying and experiencing another person in intimacy.

Treatment contracts which duplicate counter-script injunctions are especially destructive and potentially lethal contracts. The problem of "Get rid of..." contracts such as, "Don't kill yourself!", "Don't overeat!", "Don't drink!", "Don't smoke!", is that they may be counter-script injunctions, triggering automatic behavior in the form of defiance or over-adaptation with subsequent failure. That is also the problem of "Will you--I will" in-stead of...contracts. "Will" is the imperative form of the verb and is essentially a "don't think" addition to a contract.

I am aware that in interpersonal relationships in an organized society, and in situations where time is of the essence, enforced structure is essential to existence and progress. In therapy, where the long-term goal is autonomy, structure will be minimal and will refer only to the organizational items of time, place and cost of meetings. Other matters, such as behavior within the group: (apportioning time, non-violence and no sex regulations) become not authoritarian rules but rather, and properly, grist for the process mill of the group.

From Eric Berne we have inherited the ultimate permission to wrestle with, not only our personal problems but the ultimate meanings of life and relationships: the OKness of being a human being. In that belief we move alongside our mother, Psychoanalysis, and our ancestral mother, the sacred religions. To solve the dilemma, we will, however, have to rearrange some old, old patterns, particularly transference patterns.

Permission to accept my OKness as a human being is complicated by the constant presence of the transference phenomenon, not only in fact but in terminology: e.g. parent-child, teacher-pupil, doctor-patient, pastor-parishioner, lawyer-client. Our language reflects our feelings of it's not OK to be me. Is it possible to come up with a new language consistent with I am OK and You are OK?

Training, in its focus on technique, must provide an authentic atmosphere that nurtures an awareness of OKness. Examinations and Boards that are basically an ancient religious/medical model (I'm OK - You're not OK) must move to a Transactional Analysis model (It's OK with me for me to be me, and it's OK with me for you to be you,) enabling the students of Transactional Analysis to grasp, along with all the required knowledge of human behavior, a new awareness of the Right, the Respondability and the Capacity of every human being to *make decisions* and take charge of his/her own life.

More than any other criterion of special TA knowledge, this is the pivotal point on which our own fulfillment and the successful struggle of human beings rests: a clear understanding and an intellectual decision that it is OK with me for me to be me and it is OK with me for you to be you.

This is the heart of Transactional Analysis theory, and the affirmation Eric Berne handed to us for confirmation: It's OK to be HUMAN!

Eric Berne, *Games People Play*, Grove Press, New York, 1967.

Eric Berne, *Principles of Group Treatment.*, Oxford University Press, New York, 1966. On page 290, the concept of Frog-Prince is attributed to Dr. Donald Young, "who first focused my attention on Frog-Prince lore."

Thomas A. Harris, *I'm OK--You're OK*. Harperand Row, New York, 1967.

Taibi Kahler and Hedges Capers, "The Miniscript," *Transactional Analysis Journal*, 4:1, January 1974.

Claude Steiner, *Scripts People Live*. Grove Press, New York, 1974.

TWO LIFE POSITIONS

I believe that there are only two basic life positions: I am OK (I+) and I am NOT OK (I-). The I- position means that it is not OK to be me. If I see myself as NOT OK, the only clear inference is that my parent, my parent's parents, and ultimately the universe that produces us all cannot be OK. The I+ position means that it is OK for me to be me. I accept those things about me that I perceive to be unchangeable: in particular, my physical characteristics and my feelings. If I accept my own OKness in that way, I must accept the OKness of others for the same reason.

There are two ways of arriving at the OK life position: the religious affirmation and/or through an acceptance of fact. The religious stance, contrary to what institutionalized sectarian religion sometimes maintains, is that it is OK to be a human being. In the Jewish tradition this stance is symbolized in the creation story of the Book of Genesis where the creator differentiates between the value of man/woman and the rest of his creation. In the Christian tradition it is symbolized by the concept of incarnation: God living in man. If you start from a theological position of ground zero you cannot miss that declaration: it is OK to be human.

The second way of arriving at this decision is based on acceptance of fact. In the preface to his Japanese primer, Professor Nakanuma writes of the difficulty students have with the illogical structure of the Japanese language. He goes on to say, "Very well, the Japanese language is illogical, and my suggestion to those students is: learn to accept facts as they are for after all, that is all you can do." If I am dissatisfied with parts of me that I cannot change I have two options: 1) to accept myself the way I am or, 2) to refuse to accept myself the way I am and engage in a meaningless and futile conflict within for the rest of my life.

I have some handicaps and so do you: something about me that I would not have this way if I had the choice. It is an old awareness of psychology that it is easier to deal with a handicap that is visible than with a handicap that is hidden. The "heartbreak" of psoriasis is not so much in its being discovered as in the fear of it being discovered. If I have a visible handicap, say an amputated right arm, both you and I will come to terms with that handicap when in each other's presence. It is the handicap that is concealed that causes me anxiety. One set of handicaps that I carry concealed is my feelings.

I carry those feelings concealed because I have been told at an early age that I do not or should not feel what I feel. Institutions are afraid of and discourage the expression of feelings. In particular there are three sets of feelings that are discouraged: destructive feelings, sexual feelings and certain fear feelings. Consider that if you were to go about the city today with your feelings being revealed to public view, you would be arrested or hospitalized and, consider that the people who would arrest or hospitalize you would have those same feelings that you revealed!

The problem is further complicated by two fallacies: 1) denying a feeling will make it go away and 2) identifying and accepting a feeling will put it out of control. We, and our institutionalized forms of living, are afraid of feelings because of the threat of loss of control and so the persistent attempt is made to deny that such feelings are actually ours.

In actuality, denying a feeling will not make it go away. It may bury it in some repressed place where it will do untold harm emotionally, physically and socially, but it will not get rid of it. And, in fact, identifying and accepting a feeling will bring it under our conscious control. Some feelings, and anger is one of them, cannot be dealt with effectively until they are identified and accepted. For many people who suffer from emotional problems, particularly those people who are depressed this is the primary step in getting well: to discover that it is OK to feel: that it is, in fact, OK to feel anything you feel!

And so, the acceptance of my own OKness has nothing to do with how or what I feel, or what I do. My OKness has to do with the fact that I am who I am and what I am. When I accept that fact about myself, I accept that fact about you and arrive at the life position: it is OK with me for me to be me and it is OK with me for you to be you. I+ U+.

TA AND GAYS IN THE MILITARY
(A LETTER TO THE EDITOR OF "THE SCRIPT," A MONTHLY NEWSLETTER PUBLICATION OF I.T.A.A.)

DEAR Editor:

The furor raised over President Clinton's determination to lift the ban on gays being in the uniformed services was discussed in a recent 303 Study Group with the following analysis.

We began by listing our fears of allowing gays to serve in the military:

1. We might become homosexual or at least, tempted to try it.
2. They might weaken our military structure.
3. Rampant venereal disease and AIDS with high medical expense.
4. Gays might be undependable in battle.
5. Breakdown of esprit de corps.
6. A general lack of unity in the armed forces.

All of these fears stemmed from I'm NOT OK - You're NOT OK or I'm OK - You're NOT OK and none of these seemed to me to touch my basic fear.

At this point we constructed the box we live in which defines our sexual values. The sides of the box looked like this:

no sodomy

no promiscuity | no adultery

no masturbation

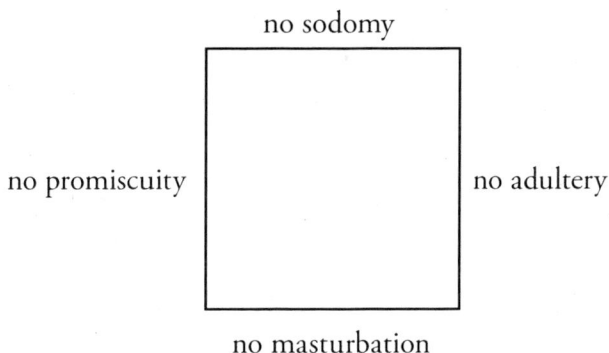

Then we looked at how airtight these values actually are in our own lives. Does no sodomy mean no oral sex? Does no masturbation mean NO masturbation? Does no promiscuity/ fornication mean none at all? Does no adultery mean absolutely no adultery? And we decided that while these limits might be alright applied to other people they applied to us only in a limited way, often atoned for by feelings of guilt. I can wink at masturbation and embrace heterosexual oral sex but I felt repulsed by male homosexual oral or anal sex This was a position of I'm OK - You're not O.K. We re-drew the box to say, NO SODOMY FOR HOMOSEXUALS, NO MASTURBA-TION FOR HOMOSEXUALS, NO PROMISCUITY FOR HOMOSEXUALS AND NO ADULTERY FOR HOMO-SEXUALS. This definitely established the basic position of I'm OK - You're not OK.

And this touched on my basic fear. I like to think that I live by the traditional box of values even though I don't hold them as absolutely authentic for my own life. And by allowing gays to openly affirm their sexuality in public I feel that I have compromised my values. I am threatened by a "hole in the dike," a weakness that may lead to a total collapse in societal values. So I am threatened by a total collapse of my world!

It is not different than my yesterday fears about allowing black and white and red and yellow integration . It is not different than my fears about allowing women to assume combat roles in wartime.

I decided to redraw my value box with only one side. My only moral restriction is that I do not violate other people. Gays and heterosexuals have the right to express their sexuality so long as they do not violate other people. That, it seems to me is I'm OK - You're Ok morality.

H. D. Johns, Rockville, Maryland

HOPE AND DESPAIR

HOPE and Despair are transactionally alike in that both involve the Adult ego state looking at the real world:

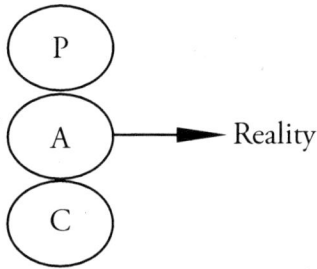

P

A   ⟶ Reality

C

In despair the Adult looks at reality and the Scared Child looking on sees the bad things of life: the natural disasters, fire and flood and earthquakes; the inhumanity of man to man, war and genocide and brutality; the discrepancies of nature, "red of tooth and claw," drought and famine, the unequal alignment of the sexes.

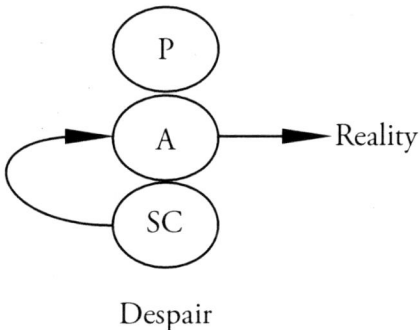

P

A   ⟶ Reality

SC

Despair

In hope the Adult looks at reality and the Free Child, looking on, sees the good things in life: the natural beauty, the blue sky and white clouds, the green grass and waterfalls, the colors of the rainbows and the birds and flowers; the warmth and love and beauty in human relationships; the opportunities to learn and grow.

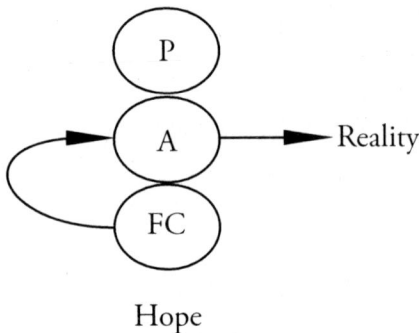

```
        ┌─────┐
        │  P  │
        └─────┘
    ┌─────┐
──▶ │  A  │ ──────▶  Reality
    └─────┘
        ┌─────┐
        │ FC  │
        └─────┘
```

Hope

The contrast is one of pessimism and optimism. The pessimism of the Scared Child scans reality and sees the worst thing scenario, the optimism of the Free Child scans the same world and sees the best case scenario. Part of reality is our interpretation of it. Seeing the glass half-empty or half-full.

Much of optimism and pessimism is superficial. That is, we scan the surface of reality and come up with a fear or a hope about what is going to happen. A cloud in the sky, although not in itself threatening, may be interpreted as forewarning a storm or promising shade on a hot sunny day. Reality stays the same, the difference lies in the inward stance. And the inward stance is in the Child ego state. A drop in the stock market may be seen, pessimistically, as predicting ruin, or optimistically, as an opportunity to buy shares of stock at a reduced price.

Superficial optimists are much happier and more pleasant to be around than superficial pessimists.

Of course, circumstances vary from place to place and

from person to person. One needs a margin in one's life to be optimistic. It is difficult to turn on the Free Child when you or your children are starving, or when floods sweep across the land or when fire destroys all that you own.

Each of us lives with fears in our Child ego state. Some of them are realistic, others have little foundation in fact. When they are not factual it is our privilege to shift our inward stance from Scared Child to Free Child. It helps to be aware that "even this" will pass. It's OK to hear the birds sing and it's OK to smell the roses. We deserve any luxury we can afford.

There is a difference between despair and depression. In depression the Parent ego state beats on the Child ego state.

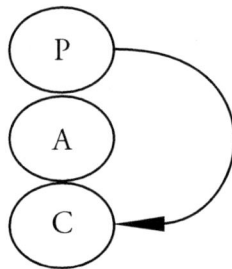

Depression

Usually some depression accompanies despair, that is, when I feel threatened by disaster, often I also feel guilty and blame myself. But despair need not accompany depression. Of the two, despair is far more serious and lethal than depression. It is looking at reality without any hope. Frequently what is diagnosed as a "clinical depression" would be more accurately defined as "despair."

INTIMACY

ERIC Berne, the founder of the system of human understanding called Transactional Analysis, wrote of 6 ways of structuring time: withdrawal, rituals, activities, pastimes, games and intimacy. Early in his writings he defined intimacy as a relationship in which none of the first five behaviors was present, and he spoke of intimacy as something fleeting and extremely rare. Later he modified this definition to include non-exploitation. My own definition of intimacy is simpler: I see it as any relationship between individuals where there is no felt threat nor exploitation. In every relationship there is both threat and exploitation. The key word is felt. When neither threat nor exploitation are felt intimacy is extant. This definition allows more experiences of intimacy in daily living and allows it to take place in any of the listed ways of structuring time with the exception of "withdrawal," in which you do not meet many interesting people. It allows intimacy to develop in "rituals," e.g. a marriage ceremony; in "activities," e.g. a quilting bee; in "pastimes," e.g. two pre-teens talking about what kind of car they want to own when they grow up; and even in games, e.g. They'll Be Glad They Know Me, in which the principal player instructs others on how to dig a well, have a baby, or plant corn.

Since most of us would like more intimacy in our primary relationships, it seems strange that we avoid it by structuring our time in the other five ways. When I am entertaining close friends I avoid intimacy by busying myself with providing food and beverages, by washing dishes as they are removed from the table and an assortment of other activities. How come? Because I am afraid to risk being rejected, or afraid of becoming so involved that I will be expected to do something that will extend my vulnerability for rejection. I can think of no other reason for avoiding intimacy.

Everyone fears rejection and one way to avoid it is to refuse offers of closeness, in some situations by rejecting the other person before he/she can reject us.

To gain intimacy it is necessary that we are aware of feelings as they are expressed in words and body language, and that we decide to express certain feelings of our own. Intimacy is experienced at the feeling level rather than the intellectual level. Two people discussing an intellectual topic may experience intimacy but that experience is felt rather than rationally exchanged. It helps to look in each other's eyes and to be aware of and give up all feelings of defensiveness. In intimacy there is no defense, only acceptance, acceptance of what the other person is saying and feeling and doing. It does not mean that I am in agreement with the other person. It only means that I accept him/her unconditionally and that I feel accepted.

Instead of being only an occasional life-sweetener intimacy can be a daily experience if we recognize our yearning for it and allow ourselves to take the risk of being close.

PHILOSOPHY

Hope as a Function of Relationship

I see Hope as one of two basic feelings. The other one is Fear. Some people have proposed a classification of four categories, corresponding closely to "glad," "sad," "angry" and "afraid." My own study indicates that fear is the underlying fuel of anger and sadness and that suggests that fear is a basic feeling category. In a corresponding way, hope, as a larger concept, can be seen to encompass "gladness" suggesting that hope is another basic feeling category. Note also that both hope and fear are feelings that are essential to the continuation of human life, i.e. without hope, or without fear, it would be impossible to remain alive.

A complete loss of hope is fatal. It is possible to be short on love and not know it. It is possible to be short on faith and never be aware of it. But it is not possible to be short on hope without being acutely aware that something is wrong with existence. To be short on hope is to be long on despair. Despair, when it is total, leads quickly to death.

One of the things that forces people into therapy is that they feel a lessening of hope. They lose a love relationship, or a job, or they feel depressed at their own perceived failures, or they sense that they are addicted to some substance, and with those circumstances they feel some despair creeping in with a decrease in their quotient of hope.

Hope is always concerned with the future but it is not a function of time. By definition, both hope and despair anticipate the future, one with positive vibrations, the other with negative ideology. I do not have to hope for what I already have (although it may be hoped that the present situation will continue into the future). Hope is an extension into the future toward what is desired. There is an expectation of fulfillment, in time. But it is not dependent upon time. Hope is not a function of time.

To think of hope as a function of time is to miss the problem of and the remedy for a person in despair. Time may heal some pain but not the pain of despair. Time may have a healing effect on the family of the dying cancer patient but it only has a deadening effect on the patient.

HOPE AS A FUNCTION OF RELATIONSHIP

Hope requires relationship or a sense of relationship. It may be diagrammed like this. (Fig. 1)

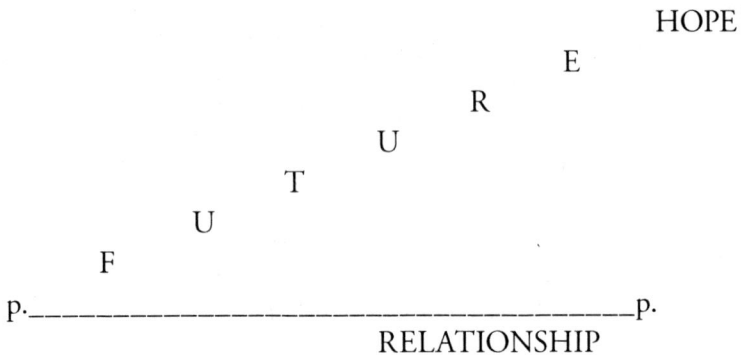

                                                    HOPE
                                          E
                                   R
                           U
                     T
               U
         F
p._____p.
                    RELATIONSHIP

(FIG. 1)HOPE as a function of relationship "p"= "person." The "Future" line is broken to indicate that it is not related to "time."

When relationship is damaged, hope is dulled. Damaged hope may be observed when there is experienced a loss, a serious illness or a forced institutionalization. When some event or trauma occurs that interrupts the consistency of the "relationship" line, there is a corresponding interruption in the "future" line. (Fig. 2.)

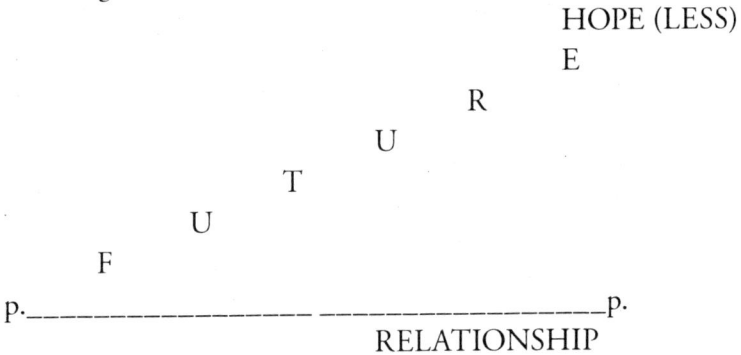

```
                                    HOPE (LESS)
                                        E
                            R
                        U
                    T
                U
        F
p._____  _____p.
                    RELATIONSHIP
```

(Fig. 2) The interruption of Relationship affects the Future and results in Hope(lessness)

The function of a therapist, or a friend, or simply another person who cares, in relieving despair (hopelessness) is to build a bridge across the fracture which has occurred in relationship. She does this in various ways: by caring, by being with, by hearing and reflecting feeling and by gentle confrontation.

BUILDING BRIDGES OF RELATIONSHIP

When hope is understood as a function of relationship, the remedial path for despair becomes clear. The remedy for despair is the building or rebuilding of relationship bridges. The is the most important dimension of a therapeutic relationship.

As a therapist or a friend you have four ways to build a relationship bridge: your presence, your caring, your hearing feeling as well as speech and your willingness to maintain an authentic atmosphere in which there is no contesting and no dilution of reality: gentle confrontation. In that authentic atmosphere a relationship bridge is built.

When relationship is enhanced, hope is enhanced. (Fig. 3)

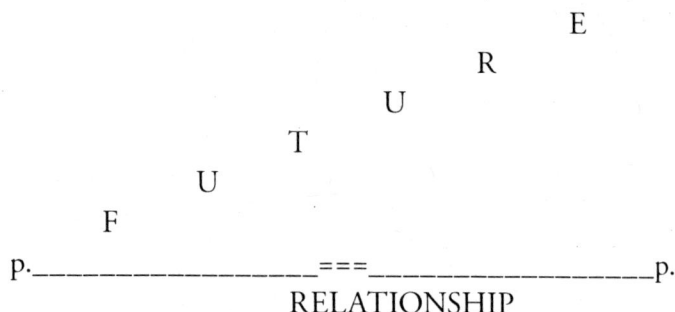

                                HOPE (FULL)

                                          E
                            R
                      U
                T
          U
      F
p._____===_____p.
                    RELATIONSHIP

(Fig. 3) Bridging the Relationship bridges the Future line and results in strengthening hope(fullness)

AN ILLUSTRATION

Martha, a 58 year-old housewife, hospitalized for two years with a diagnosis of Clinical Depression, refused to speak in the first two session with her new therapist. She hunched, trembling, in her chair. Here is the gist of what the therapist said as he occasionally broke the long periods of silence in the first three interviews.

"Martha, I know you must have lots of mixed feelings about being here. Part of you would like to stay where you are. Part of you would like to change...

"I see you as living behind a huge pile of rocks. It's dark and comfortable back there because you don't have to take on a lot of responsibilities...

"I'd like you to move out into the sunlight a little way, Martha. I'm not going to push you--I'm going to nudge you a little. You're strong enough to move a little. You don't have to take on that big load of responsibilities all at once...

"I know it's frightening out here Martha. If you decide to move out into the sunlight, what would be the first thing

you'd like to be strong enough to do?...
"You're feeling like the risk is just too much: it takes so much energy...
"Forget about that big stack of responsibilities for awhile, forget about that big responsibility, you don't have to do that until you're ready...
"I know the effort seems just too much. As you move out a bit, you'll find your strength is returning enough to do what you'd like to do...

During the fourth session, Martha spoke for the first time, saying, "It takes so much energy." During the sixth session, she spoke of the things she "ought" to do, and when the therapist replied that he didn't like "oughts," she smiled for the first time. At the beginning of the seventh session, she said, "I baked a cake." The therapist asked her to tell him about that, and she replied, "It takes too much energy, you just don't know how much energy it takes."

Therapist: "It takes a lot of energy to think about all those things you "ought" to do. You don't have to do anything you're not ready to do. Nobody's going to push you.

In that therapeutic setting a relationship was bridged and Martha recovered a sense of hope. She recovered sufficiently to enjoy limited activities with family and friends before the therapist learned what had caused and what had precipitated her loss of hope. That traumatic event, linked with her past, was revealed in time. It was not necessary to go into that initially, nor would it have been profitable. Martha recovered her hope through her relationship with the therapist.

1. This 4-fold classification has been attributed to Muriel James. I have never seen it in print. I have often asked students to classify feelings and invariably they have come up with these four.

2. Johns, H. D., "Three Pots of Anger," Transactional Analysis Journal 4:3, July 1974.

3. When anger is manifested one of ten fear-threats can be detected: feeling anxious, frustrated, overwhelmed, hurt, excluded, discounted, disappointed, cheated, embarrassed, violated.

4. Despair may be described in Transactional Analysis terms as I'm not OK, You're not OK. In Eric Berne's words, "You don't see much of these people except in a hospital or in the morgue." Notes, Summer Conference, Monterey, California, 1965.

5. Gentle confrontation is confronting only with the reality that is perceived as capable of being substantiated and from the I'm OK, You're OK position.

6. Martha (not her real name) was not suffering from depression but from despair. Depression is not fatal. Despair is. For the difference, see Eric Berne, Principles of Group Treatment, (New York: Oxford University Press, 1966) p. 278.

LESSONS IN PATIENCE

God, grant me the serenity to accept the things I cannot change
the courage to change the things I can,
and the wisdom to know the difference.
                                                    -Anonymous

THESE words hang framed in my office where I see them every day but it was not until a summer day in Japan that I came to know what they really mean. These words speak not only of wisdom and courage, they speak of patience. They say that patience is a major part of wisdom.

The Tofukuji Temple in Kyoto is an ancient temple devoted to the practice of Zen. Although there is no simple definition of Zen, its practice certainly involves the ideals of patience, acceptance and serenity. One June day I spent an important morning of my life talking with an ancient priest of Zen Buddhism in his living quarters within the compound of Tofukuji. For more than two hours we discussed the philosophy of Zen and the similarities and differences in Eastern and Western thought, but the conversation grew tiring because of the difficulties of translation and the oriental mystery of Zen.

I sat on the tatami facing a beautiful garden and found my concentration slipping away to fasten on a stone lantern which stood a little apart from a small group of pines and shrubs. It was a lovely old lantern but it had a flaw about it. One of the shelf stones had been tipped ever so slightly to one side, giving an overall imbalance to an otherwise perfect picture. Although I did not recognize the actual imbalance in the picture I was seeing, I suddenly realized as I looked and listened to the venerable old priest that I was trying to straighten my mental image of the lantern--to make it erect and completely perfect in my mind's eye. In so doing I was fastening my attention not upon the beauty of the lantern but upon my own need to set it straight.

Although this did not tell me what Zen is, it certainly spoke of what Zen is not!

In the afternoon we were taken by Mr. Tanaka, a serious devotee of Zen, to visit the Katsuura Detached Imperial Palace, a scene which few westerners have had the opportunity of seeing, and one which many Japanese in Kyoto would never be able to see. It was Mr. Tanaka's first visit, also.

But it was raining and all during the lunch hour I worried about the rain spoiling the obvious pleasure that our host was having in showing us the lovely views of Kyoto. I reckoned without Mr. Tanaka's patience. For we saw the Katsuura Detached Palace and we saw it in the rain. And rather than apologize for the inconvenience of the rain, Mr. Tanaka obviously found the experience enhanced by the realization that we were having a treat made more rare by the softness of the color-tones in the beautiful garden of the detached palace--a softness which was the direct result of the overcast sky like a picture slightly under exposed so that the colors are rich and full. So the Katsuura Detached Palace stood out on this rainy afternoon. And Mr. Tanaka and we walked and relaxed in this lovely garden in the rain without an apology or a complaint. "God, grant me the serenity to accept with such esthetic participation the things I cannot change."

So that afternoon I learned a lesson I shall not forget. A

lesson in patience as taught by Mr. Tanaka, a busy man, who had taken an afternoon to show his American guests a lovely view and was not disturbed by an imperfection in the day.

There is one more chapter to this story. Before going to Japan I had studied conversational Japanese and I began a formal study of the language in Japan. At first I found myself quite upset by inconsistencies in Japanese Grammar. And then, one evening, I re-read the preface to Professor Nakanuma's *Basic Japanese Grammar*. In that introduction he said an amazingly simple thing that ties the threads of this story together. It was this. Said Professor Naganuma, "...the Japanese language is sometimes inconsistent. My suggestion ...is, learn to accept facts as they are, for after all, that is the only thing you can do."

Such is the art of patience. I hope I shall continue to learn it because I am convinced that the words of an ancient Japanese proverb are necessary to a serene life: "Five pounds of patience are worth a bushel of brains."

The Dilemma of Good and Evil

When George Burns, in the role of God in the movie "Oh God!" spoke of the mistakes of creation, he cited the size of the avocado seed as an example. "I made the avocado seed too big," he said. In that humorous vignette there is a glaring truth. It only seems subtle because we have been programmed not to see reality as it surrounds us. The truth in that statement is not a matter of whether the avocado seed actually is too big. There is no way to check that kind of reality. The glaring truth revealed in the statement is that the human mind is surprised when it first witnesses cutting into an avocado and sees the size of the seed. It is the same kind of surprise we experience when first we come face-to-face with an experience of nature's "redness of tooth and claw:" we are surprised and, frankly, we don't like the truth of what we see.

There are several huge dilemmas in human experience which have to do with this discrepancy in the way we perceive things should be and the way they actually are. We would have a world where food supplies are plentiful. Contrast that with the underfed millions in our world. We would have an earth safe from the ravages of fire and flood and earthquake. Contrast that yearning with the facts: everyday news headlines catalogue the natural disasters that frequent our world.

We would make man and woman compatible with each other in their perceptions and their emotions. A 50 percent divorce rate in this country belies that hope. I have been a therapist for thirty years during which time I have dealt with hundreds of cases of sexual affairs outside the primary relationship bonding. Yet, if you define monogamy as the yearning for one person who will satisfy all my needs and for whom I will do the same, I have never known a human being who did not aspire to monogamy. Think of this horrendous discrepancy: every man and woman aspiring to monogamy, no human beings who actually are monogamous.

If you think that is an over-statement research it for yourself. Start with yourself. You may live monogamously. Many people do. Some with happiness and fulfillment. Yet all are, or can be seduced to be, subject to temptation. From this viewpoint the amazing thing is not the rampant sexual revolution of the sixties, seventies and eighties. The amazing thing is that vast number of people who aspire to sexual monogamy--millions of people hoping for a monogamous relationship and very little monogamy in actual practice.

Part of this dilemma is rooted in an anatomical discrepancy. Sexologists have begun to enunciate clearly the anatomical problem of coital disparity. A man and a woman do not fit together in intercourse as we think they should, so that the vast majority of women do not experience orgasm during coitus. Note again that the discrepancy is between what our aspirations are and what the facts turn out to be.

When you turn from nature to the man-made structures of society you discover the same discrepancies between aspirations and the way things are. When Thomas Jefferson spoke of the value of the "least" government it was because he divined the truth about governmental structures: they tend to defeat the purpose for which they are designed. Of course, all institutions do that. A great idea is pronounced. People are impressed by it and gather about it and promote it. They institutionalize it. And it never again has the power of its origin because it has been locked up in a self-perpetuating structure. Even language holds this problem. It tends to defeat the purpose of communication. Walk around this dilemma for a moment. We know of no way to maintain and sustain a culture without structure. And yet structure tends to defeat the cultural design. Perhaps it is what Kant had in mind when he said that every idea contains within itself the seed of its own destruction. What a discrepancy that is!

But in all of these discrepancies there is a greater dilemma. When human beings recognized that reality was at odds with their aspirations they began to look for reasons and they came up with what is probably the most destructive concept of human history. They conceived the idea of GOOD and EVIL. If such entities exist then it must follow that things can be categorized as good or evil and if things can be so categorized, then obviously the people who do those things can be categorized in the same way. In other words, when we experience a discrepancy between our aspirations and things as they are we are programmed by thousands of years of usage to look for the evil and the evil one.

The first victim of that nomenclature is the self. Although we disguise it with several standard ego-defense mechanisms most of us suspect that "I" am the one that is not OK. Again, most of us learn to disguise that low self-image and project the negative images onto other people. If there is evil then somebody must carry the blame: I, or you, or perhaps, they.

See the dilemma again. Confronted with discrepancy in our aspirations and the way things are, we see the disharmony as evil and pronounce it as evil. We then go out to wage war with evil and, although human history by the book seems to be making some gains, human history by the page is a sad story of humiliating defeat. For thousands of years we have done battle with the wrong foe. Evil is an elusive foe. Indeed, as an entity, it does not exist!

We can begin by accepting reality, the harsh facts as well as the beautiful facts, for what they are. The bird singing in the maple tree just outside my door is not singing to the glory of God and the universe. He is staking out his sexual territory and he can be brutal in his defense of that territory.

We move toward a compassionate understanding of our world when we admit that the song of the bird is an illusion. We admit that we live by illusions, by our hopes for a world where birds sing. And we admit that part of reality is in our perception of it. And we continue to hope.

In other words it is OK to interpret the whistling of the bird as song while knowing that it is not song. It is OK to interpret marriage as a foundation for happiness while knowing that for a large part of the population it is a basis for less than that. It is OK to eat avocados while acknowledging that the size of the seed surprises us.

But what about the criminal activity in our societies? Surely the criminal element is an evil. We aspire to a world free of such frightening forces. At any rate, that calls for remedy rather than acceptance! Of course it does, and what we are saying here is that that remedy must begin by ceasing to categorize the men and women who do evil as evil people and see them for what they are--men and women who are driven to do evil deeds through fear.

Here is a thief. What drives him to steal? Fear of his own inadequacy as it surfaces in frustration, hurt, exclusion, discounting, disappointment, feeling cheated or embarrassed. Or a rapist, again driven by fear of inadequacy. Or terrorists, and again we see the driving force of fears.

What we are saying is that we are not dealing well with thieves and rapists and terrorists by thinking of them in terms of evil. There is hope in beginning to think of them in terms of speaking and acting to their fears.

Or perhaps, closer to home, what about the evil done us

by family members, friends or colleagues at work? We want the goodwill of those about us. A brother acts hostile toward me? I can call him "evil" or I can see beneath the evil to the fear that drives his hostility, and speak to it, "I hear you feeling frustrated, or hurt, or cheated," etc., rather than replying defensively and thus triggering another round of hostility.

Above all, we can accept our own fears as fears rather than evils. By so doing we do not get rid of the fears, but accepting them makes them play with a dimmer voice and enables us to communicate without the verbal defense that sets up threat in the other person.

Our enemy is FEAR. Men do evil not because they are evil but because they are afraid. If you say that there is evil alive in this universe, I say you are going down the same futile path that mankind has followed since they grasped onto the tragic concept. Theologians have argued the problem of evil for centuries, not from a ground-zero-base of, "Does it exist?" but from a reductio ad absurdum stance of "Why does God allow it to exist and from where did it originate?" It seems to me that the only light at the end of the long and dark tunnel is to recognize that the enemy is not evil but fear, the fear that comes from the discrepancies that we may never understand but never-the-less are fact. That, at least would free mankind from the dismal burden of evil and allow us to get on with how we can live, and be, and enjoy, in a world where things do not always make sense.

MEANS AND ENDS

MEANS and ends are interdependent. That is, when you focus on one you determine the other. Choose destructive ends, you will use destructive means to achieve them. The choice of constructive means leads to constructive ends. The only negation of this rule is this: you may focus on a constructive end but if you use destructive means to achieve it you will inevitably compromise the results.

The oldest fallacy of man still generally in practice is that "The end justifies the means." The idea that if the goal is good, it is OK to use whatever methods are necessary to achieve it is in practice in most institutions: in families, in churches, in schools, in prisons, in hospitals and probably most of all in almost all forms of government.

Consider how it is practiced in families. The goal of most parents is that our children grow up to be happier and more successful than we are. To achieve that end what means do we employ? Most of us, unwilling to see our children suffer pain over-indulge them; unwilling to have them make mediocre grades in school do at least part of their homework for them; unwilling to see them fail at anything, heap guilt upon them. Thus our children grow up less than self-sufficient and with a less than satisfactory self-image.

Consider how it is practiced in prisons. The aim of incarceration is expressed as rehabilitation. The means used are non-educative and debasing. So the rate of recidivism is to be expected. We use violent means to discourage violence when it is pretty well understood that violence breeds violence.

Consider how it is practiced in national politics. We can accept the ideal that most governmental officials pursue office out of a sense of urgency to make a positive difference in the state of the nation. In order to finance their pursuit, however, they form alliances with power structures. They salve their consciences with the logical explanation that without financial help they can't possibly win the office and help the national cause. Once they have gained office the means they used to get there has a powerful influence on the ends which they promote.

Consider how it is practiced in international relations. The United States sees itself as the instigator and preserver of democratic processes throughout the world. When, then, we see a nation that practices civil abuse toward its citizenry, what do we do? Of course, we bring force to bear upon that nation, either through economic sanctions or military threat. Neither of these encourage democracy because both of them are oppressive. Nowhere is this more obvious than in the infamous Iran-contra affair in which United States-manufactured arms were sold to Iran with the purpose of financing South American Freedom-Fighters. What was wrong with that? In the first place it furthered the enmity between the United States and Iran by the huge profits Iran was forced to pay for illicit arms, teaching that country that that was the way successful nations conduct business. In the second place by furnishing finances for the contras we endorsed the killing of those who disagree with us.

War itself does not solve problems. It only postpones the reactionary antagonism, perhaps for fifty or even for a hundred years. In the meantime, those who stand by and watch learn how to force their will on those with whom they disagree.

"The end justifies the means" is probably the greatest fallacy of all human endeavor. Most people suspect there is a flaw in that philosophy. Yet most of us use it as an excuse for behaviors that otherwise would be unacceptable. It is far more true that "the means determines the end."

SPIRITUALITY

IN 1974 I introduced what I then called the Perspicacity Formula but which has come to be known as the Autonomy Formula:

$$I - Rt + Rsd + C \text{ to make decisions} + TCOL$$

Every Individual (I) has the Right (Rt), the Respondability (Rsd), and the Capacity (C) to make decisions ( ) and Take Charge of his/her Own Life (TCOL).

In this formula, in keeping with the then current emphasis, I stressed the right of the individual to make decisions and take charge of his/her own life. That was the emphasis of the sixties, the seventies and the eighties. During these three decades there was a shift in the apparent values of the American public, at least in the media: television, magazines, moving pictures. This change in apparent values seeped into the cultural institutions of family, school and church. Along with these changes came a renewed emphasis on the rights of the self: assertive (usually interpreted as "aggressive") rights, a shift from the "we" to the "I." This, in turn, was accompanied by an increase in violence and crime. The emphasis was on the "I" and the OKness of anger and people were encouraged to express their anger: to "let it out!"

Now there is concern for what has happened and is happening in America and a growing feeling that we need a return to traditional values: nurturing families with the full-time presence of a parent; discipline in our schools; and even a renewed emphasis on religious practice, church attendance, prayer in schools, morality in our governmental agents. All three of these traditional values are probably impossible to attain. There is, however, some hope if we begin to practice, individually, the second element in the Autonomy Formula: Respondability.

Respondability is a coined term meaning the willingness to respond , rather than react, to stimuli and the acceptance of responsibility for our individual and at least some of our collective behavior. This means a concern for values.

To respond to stimuli rather than react to stimuli involves challenging a false belief: that anger needs to be expressed as anger, i.e., aggressivity. The expression of anger invites violence and irresponsibility. We cannot will away our angry feeling but we can control our angry behavior in a responsible way. We can, instead of expressing anger, express ourselves assertively. Anger is always fueled by fear. Assertiveness is fueled by fear and hope, with decision. When we control our angry behavior by decision we mitigate our angry feelings. Decisive action is the result of a sequence of events. Feelings in the Child ego state are examined by the value systems in the Parent ego state and a decision is made in the Adult ego state, thus:

Rights are perceived by the C, Responsibility is a function of the P, and Capacity and Responses by Decision are found only in the A.

A concern for values is one definition of spirituality. Values are those things we care for most. We are spiritual when we grow quiet like deep pools in the presence of the highest and best that we know and when we enable ourselves and others to think on planes of ultimate meaning.

The fundamental question of spirituality is this: does life, with its intricacies, evolve by accident or does it have some inherent purpose? Are the things we care for most: love, hope, beauty, warmth at the random mercy of the things we care for least: brutality, fear, ugliness, coldness of thought? If life evolves by accident there may be some short-term values to be gained but there is little of ultimate value to be gained in contemplation. If it has purpose there is meaning in the search for ultimate values.

STRUCTURE

In the aftermath of every great discovery, those who believe in it are faced with a dilemma. The dilemma is how to preserve, protect and promote the value of the discovery without defeating it. Usually the second generation of believers institutionalize the idea. They build a box: a creed or covenant, a code of conduct or a statement of essentials. Then policies are established to protect the box. In the ensuing fear of heresy, people become less and less important until finally the idea is lost in the need for commitment to it. Thus, institutions tend to defeat the purpose for which they are designed.

Consider the great idea of human welfare. The idea is that every human individual is entitled to adequate food, clothing and shelter, and today in most of the advanced nations of the world, medical attention. We have given structure to that idea. And in so doing have tended to rob the indigent people of initiative so that welfare becomes a normal way of life for them. Instead of promoting the value of human individuality the institutionalization of that idea tends to defeat it.

Religion is an example of how such destruction takes place. The great religions are founded on some variation of the Golden Rule: "Do unto others as you would have them do unto you." Yet most of the conflicts between groups of people have their roots in competition between institutionalized religions. So structured education tends to defeat the purpose of education: to enable each individual to be creatively useful and happy in the daily tasks of living. And even Language tends to clutter the landscape of communication.

On the other hand, structure is essential to our living. We have never figured out how to transmit a culture without institutionalizing it, placing it in a box.

Without structure, everyone would go his own way, do his own thing and the result would be complete disorder.

Consider, however, that every attempt to place structure into any given situation arises out of feelings of inadequacy. Without structuring our time we would be at the mercy of whimsy. Impulsivity would take over our lives and lead us to certain ruin. How could a physician see patients without scheduling them by the time-clock? How could commerce be carried on without defining a time and place for the work-day?

There is no solution to this dilemma. There is, however, a way of countering it: by maintaining the uncomfortable openness of sitting on the point of decision in every policy matter. The point of decision looks like this:

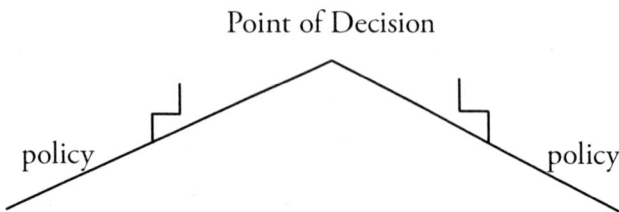

Point of Decision

policy   policy

On either side of the point there is an easy chair called "policy." Policies, of course, are for protection of the institution. When a policy is in effect no thinking about people or situations is necessary. In fact, all that is needed is "commitment" to the institution that has been established. There is less and less need for decision and less and less need for investment. This is also more comfortable than sitting on the point of decision.

To provide that kind of structure requires injunctions that support the institution and discount one factor of the other person's OKness. To discount one's right to make decisions invites passivity. To discount one's responsibility to make decisions invites dependency. To discount one's capacity to make decisions invites one to feel inept and fragmented.

Structure is essential to our living. Yet it tends to rob us of one of these factors of our autonomy. I am deeply troubled by the institutionalization of any great idea. It always tends to defeat the purpose for which the institution was designed. Instead of policies and commitments I propose the less concrete and more risky plan of decisions and investments. For after all:

- Policies are for insurance. (Life, Accident, Liability)
- Commitment is for institutions. (Hospitals, Prisons, Marriage)

while

- Decisions are for getting on and,
- Investments are for getting rich.

GETTING THERE
(THE PATHWAY TO ARRIVING)

IN Carlos Castaneda's *The Teachings of Don Juan* (1968, Berkeley, University of California Press) don Juan gives a road map for arriving at power and knowledge. (It is the one thing I find extremely important in Castaneda's writing.) He speaks of four "enemies" and says that in "defeating" these four, one becomes a "man of knowledge." (pp.56 ff.)

The four enemies are, in order, Fear, Clarity, Power and Aging. I place a different "spin" on these four enemies. I see them not as being vanquished: they remain in one's life forever. Instead of defeating them, I see the pathway advancing as one comes to deal successfully with them. In learning to deal with them, each one in turn, becomes my friend and never again will be my enemy.

The first enemy everyone faces in arriving at knowledge about life is Fear. Fear-threat is the most destructive element in our attempt to communicate with others. It manifests itself in defensive behavior instead of hearing the feeling and meaning coming from the other person and thus fosters reaction instead of response. When it goes unrecognized it quickly escalates into Anger resulting again in reactive behavior, either over-adaptation or submission/withdrawal. It is a blockage in our pathway to understanding and compassion which are necessary steps in arriving at knowledge. Fear-threat is constantly our companion. Two major feelings of threat are (1) the fear of failing and (2) the fear of the loss of selfness (often felt as "being cheated.") We feel some minimum fear-threat in everything we feel and think and do. When we drive a car, we are constantly under threat, when we transact business or cook a meal or write a letter, we feel the threat of failing or the threat of the loss of our selfness.

We never vanquish fear. People who are "cured" of phobias are acutely aware of that. We move out in spite of our fears to make decisions and get on with our lives. And in so-doing we discover that fear becomes our friend. It stands guard against our suffering harm and humiliation. So we accept it, embrace it and it becomes our life-long friend, and never again will it be our enemy. We have taken the first step toward arriving.

And we immediately run into our second enemy: Clarity. Clarity mounts on a pedestal and spotlights my picture of how things are and how they should be. When we see a pathway clearly, be it our own or that of another person, we have no doubt of what should be done and timing becomes paramount. We may either rush in to solve the problem or sit back smugly and do nothing. Coupled with that is the fact that although we understand and see solutions clearly, we may be wrong, particularly when we are dealing with another person's problem. The temptation is to coach, rather than counsel, to solve the problem, rather than to encourage the other person to solve his own problem. A third danger presented by clarity is that having gained it, we stop reaching for new knowledge and stay precisely where we are. When we have conquered the temptations to misuse it, have learned to be patient and to consider carefully each decisive step, clarity will never again be our enemy. It becomes our life-long friend. It introduces us to our third enemy, Power.

When we sense that we see clearly, we become potent: we feel invincible. We tend to become demanding. We take risks. We walk in the paths of danger. Such a sense of power can turn us into cruel beings who violate the boundaries of other people. When we come to terms with potency, and turn it into constructive rather than destructive behavior, it becomes our friend. It enables us to walk erectly and assertively at all times. It enables us to express our fears , to expose our weaknesses and explore our strengths. It enables us to face our fourth enemy without excessive agitation. Our fourth enemy is Aging.

Aging, that inevitable process of growing old, is never conquered. But having dealt successfully with our fears, our clarity and our potency we can face successfully our struggle between resting and moving on. There are, of course, times for resting. Such times come often among our periods of struggle, Part of successful living is found in struggle and part of it is found in retreat and recuperation. The person who has moved from enmity to friendship with his Fears, his Clarity and his Potency can decide when to struggle and when to rest.

One reason that Aging is hard to deal with is that it arrives as a surprise. I do not expect it until dawns upon me that it is happening to me, so I am unprepared for its onset. But having learned to deal with Fear, I confront my Aging. Having learned to cope with Clarity, I see the advantages and disadvantages of my aging process clearly. Having learned the reasonable limits of my Power, I submit to Aging and its inevitable result. Thus in this last stage of the pathway as in the preparation for it I have arrived!

INDEX

ISBN 1-41206062-1